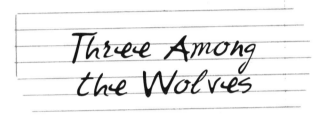

Three Among the Wolves

Three Among the Wolves

A COUPLE AND THEIR DOG LIVE A YEAR
WITH WOLVES IN THE WILD

HELEN THAYER

SASQUATCH BOOKS
SEATTLE

To the wolves who became our friends
To Charlie who made it all possible

Printed in Canada
Published by Sasquatch Books
Distributed by Publishers Group West
12 11 10 09 08 07 06   9 8 7 6 5 4 3 2 1

Book design: Stewart A.Williams
Cover photographs: © Eric Coia / Dreamstime.com (center image)/
    Helen and Bill Thayer (all others)
Interior photographs: Helen and Bill Thayer
Map: Marge Mueller

Library of Congress Cataloging-in-Publication Data is available.

ISBN 1-57061-479-2

Sasquatch Books / 119 South Main Street, Suite 400 / Seattle, WA 98104 /
206/467-4300
www.sasquatchbooks.com
custserv@sasquatchbooks.com

Contents

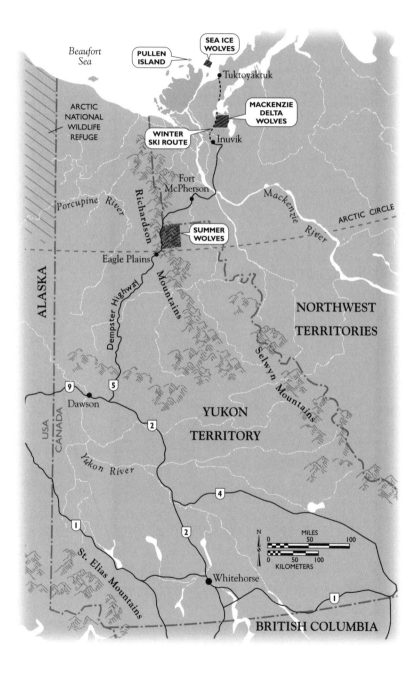

Introduction

ALONE IN THE WILDERNESS of the Canadian Yukon, my husband Bill and I zigzagged up a steep slope to a knife-edged ridge. After discarding our packs, we crouched among lichen-covered boulders to scan our binoculars across a remote meadow nestled in the valley below. Our hearts skipped a beat when we spotted them: two wolves, one black and one blond. The pair strolled into the open. Three more adults and four roly-poly pups soon joined them. Charlie, our part-wolf canine companion, stood unseen on a short leash at our side, silent and still, his gaze fixed on the pack. Undetected downwind, we three continued our secret watch.

The black wolf, gripping a large stick between his teeth, began an energetic tug-of-war with the pups while the other four wolves flopped down in what seemed to be favorite places. After a few minutes the black wolf joined the rest of the pack, leaving the pups' game to deteriorate into a raging fight. A dark gray wolf darted out and, with a few well-placed nips on rears, ended the squabble. The chastised pups scurried behind the rocks into their den.

From the trampled meadow, a heavily used trail, embedded in the tundra, snaked into a grove of stunted spruce trees. Two more trails switchbacked to the rocky summit of a steep slope. The den we had been seeking for the past eight weeks was dug into its base.

As Bill and I rejoiced at our discovery, howls suddenly erupted from the distant tundra beyond the trees. All the wolves jumped to their feet to stare in the direction of the sound, waving their tails expectantly. Soon five more adults emerged from the trees, dragging behind them the partly eaten carcass of a white Dall sheep. The pack greeted the hunters excitedly, licking their muzzles. A large male regurgitated partly digested meat for the pups, while the rest of the family ripped apart and eagerly consumed the sheep. After eating his fill, the black wolf climbed to the summit and sat with his back to us.

As we counted the wolves—sixteen altogether—Charlie tugged at his leash and took a step forward. Pointing his muzzle to the sky, he gave a long howl. The black wolf leaped to his feet and spun to face Charlie, who dropped silently to his belly, laying his head on his paws. He kept his eyes below those of the wolf, looking downward to display submission and respect.

We expected the wolf to retreat out of caution, but instead he returned Charlie's howl. The blond wolf sped up the trail to the black one's side. Now both stared at Charlie.

Charlie raised his muzzle and howled again. The pair stood tall and alert, with tails curled above their backs. In unison, both returned Charlie's call. Then they bounded downhill to rejoin their pack. The rest of the wolf family was guarded but calm, watching Charlie, who gazed back, relaxed but vigilant.

Still hidden, Bill whispered, "We should leave."

To mark the den's location on our map, we quickly took a reading with our global positioning system (GPS). Then we crouched low and began to creep away silently, still downwind. Charlie followed at first, then stopped to look back. With an urgent tug of his leash I whispered, "Come on." We didn't stop or straighten up until we were well out of sight.

After two more miles of trekking across steep slopes and uneven tundra, we arrived at our camp, where we took another position reading to record our tent site in our journal notes. We would use these readings to locate the den when we returned next summer, equipped and ready to attempt to live among these wondrous creatures.

🐾

In our thirty-two years of marriage, Bill and I had worked together on more than twenty expeditions. He was a helicopter pilot who had amassed almost 13,000 flight hours during a career spanning four countries: New Zealand, the dense jungles of Guatemala and Honduras, and the United States, where he was a bush pilot in Alaska's mountains. My love of outdoor adventure had begun early, at nine years of age, when I began climbing mountains in my home country of New Zealand. As I grew older, I challenged myself with more technical routes and also competed as a discus thrower for New Zealand, Guatemala, and the United States. Later, in 1975, I won the U.S. national luge championship and represented the United States in European competition.

But the mountains were my first love. In 1986 I decided to embark on a series of expeditions to the world's remote regions. Journeys with Bill included kayaking 1,200 miles through the Amazon rain forest and trekking 2,400 miles through the Sahara Desert. Closer to our home in the northwestern United States, we had explored 1,500 miles of the Mojave and Sonoran Deserts. In 1997 I trekked solo in Antarctica, and Bill and I walked 1,450 miles across the Gobi Desert of Mongolia in 2001.

In 1988, in celebration of my fiftieth birthday, I became the first woman ever to complete a solo trek to the magnetic North Pole. The trek was just one element of my quest to create a continuing educational series called Adventure Classroom that would enable me to share the challenges and wonders of the world with students of all ages, worldwide, through websites, lectures, and books.

The success of the first program encouraged me to join with Bill in a second journey on foot to the Pole four years later,

*The Richardson Mountains where we hope to find a wolf den,
as viewed from Eagle Plains.*

again without dog teams or snowmobiles. Between these two polar journeys, we spent many months exploring remote areas in Alaska and in Canada's Yukon Territory, the Northwest Territories, and Nunavut, where we encountered repeated examples of wolves coexisting with other creatures. Seeing such cooperation piqued our curiosity.

As we trekked with caribou during their spring migration in Alaska, for instance, we observed wolves following the Western Arctic caribou herd as the almost half-million animals streamed north to their calving grounds on the North Slope. Similarly, in Canada we watched wolves following the Porcupine caribou herd as they traveled about four hundred miles from the Canadian Yukon to their calving area in Alaska's Arctic National Wildlife Refuge. During previous expeditions in the northern polar regions, we had observed wolves and arctic foxes following polar bears in apparent harmony with each other.

I had been fascinated by wolves for many years, but it was Bill who really began studying wolves in the wild. While flying a helicopter as a commercial bush pilot in Alaska, he had seen many wolves at their dens and watched them as they pursued prey across the tundra, and had developed a lasting respect for the animals. Although usually soft-spoken and somewhat reserved, he had felt compelled to speak to Alaskan government agencies repeatedly concerning the need to protect wolves from aerial hunters, who sought to destroy entire wolf families by shooting them from planes. As his protests continued to go unheeded, he became even more determined to work toward a better understanding of wolves and their environmental importance.

These experiences led us to dream of a new program for Adventure Classroom, one in which we would explore the intertwined relationship of the gray wolf species (*Canis lupus*) and the other animals who share the wolf's habitat, from grizzly bears to caribou. Gray wolves inhabit parts of North America, Europe, and Asia. A symbol of the wilderness, they are astute hunters, socially complex, family oriented, with strong nurturing instincts—in many ways like our good friend the dog, but also cannily like humans. Perhaps our similarities are the reason wolves have often taken center stage in the human imagination and today stir strong emotional debate over their place in the world.

We conceived of a yearlong project in which we would attempt to live close to wild wolves, to share their home range, to feel their emotions and observe their lifestyle. Our main goal was to gain greater insight, over a summer, into wolves' food-sharing habits with land-bound animals such as grizzlies and ravens. Then, the following winter, we hoped to observe the same behavior among wolves, polar bears, and foxes.

Due to the extreme difficulty of studying wild wolves up close at their dens and on hunts for a lengthy period, little of the wolves' food-sharing behavior has been documented. Radio collars and airplanes have allowed some study of this elusive animal, and respected, hardworking biologists such as Adolph Murie, David Mech, Rick McIntyre, Diane Boyd, and Renee Askins have gained valuable knowledge from years of following wild wolf tracks and studying other clues. Their research has informed our own study of wolves in the wild.

Much of the scientific knowledge about wolves comes from the study of captive animals, however, and studying managed packs has many drawbacks. No matter how well an enclosure is set up, the wolves still live within wire fences, a barrier to their innermost emotions and survival skills. They cannot use their considerable intelligence and inherited knowledge to find prey and return it to the den after a nightlong hunt. A pack in captivity must always be managed. If abandoned, its social order disintegrates, tensions rise, and members often die or are killed. In contrast, wild wolves depend on instinct and experience to establish ranking and boundaries, and only in their natural environment can wolves interact with other species.

We had no interest in raising or studying wolves in captivity. Our experience would have to come in the wolves' home range, according to their own boundaries and rules. But how could we possibly camp close enough to a den to observe and photograph a family? Wolves' secretive nature would likely make them vanish at the first sign of humans. We would have to find a wild pack, discover its den, and gain the group's trust. Then we would try to spend an entire summer with them. Later we would attempt an expedition to observe wolves in the Arctic for more than three winter months.

Wildlife scientists told us the goals of our summer and winter expeditions were sound, but gaining a wild pack's trust could be an impossible challenge. One day while visiting a wolf rescue center near our home in Washington State, Bill and I spoke to one of the keepers about our plans. When I mentioned Charlie and his upbringing, the keeper suggested that Charlie might be the answer to our problem. The more we thought about the idea, the more it made sense to us. Charlie's paternal family included a wild arctic gray wolf who entered the picture three generations ago. This ancestor was a member of the same species as the Yukon wolves, *Canis lupus*. The rest of his kin were Canadian Eskimo huskies, an Arctic sled-dog breed said to be distantly linked to wolves: intelligent, hard working, loyal, and easily trained. The combination of this remarkable breed and his wolf genes, although distant, gave Charlie a distinct edge in the wilderness.

The Inuit people from whom I bought Charlie had raised him not only around polar bears but near wolves, so he felt completely at ease with these distant cousins. Some wolves, in fact, even took shelter under the settlement buildings where Charlie was raised and had foraged for scraps. Until our dogs back home in the Cascade Range of Washington taught him to bark, he had howled like a wolf. As he and I had returned from the Pole, I watched him romp with year-old gray wolves on the sea ice.

Not only that, Charlie was a natural alpha—the leader of the pack. At home, he dominated our other dogs. Even the donkeys, goats, alpacas, and cats treated him with a level of respect that they never extended to each other. He was their undisputed leader.

Perhaps we could depend on Charlie's insight into wolf life, his inherited wolf nature, and his proud alpha bearing—which resembled the best of wolf behavior—to impress a wild wolf family and earn its respect. Perhaps Charlie would be able to communicate with a wild pack as he had with his Arctic playmates. If he could bridge the gap, we might be able to make new discoveries about wolves' hidden lives. If a wolf family accepted him as our alpha leader, regarding Bill and me as his pack, they might permit us to camp close enough to their den for our study.

Charlie weighs almost 100 pounds, making him smaller than some male wolves, who can weigh as much as 120 pounds.

He has a black, wolflike coat with white paws, a white chest, and a white-flecked muzzle. Unlike a wolf's ears, which stand up, the tips of Charlie's ears flop over, a trait he inherited from his mother. He has a typical Eskimo husky chest, which is considerably broader than that of an average wolf. Although always the boss, Charlie's nature is very doglike, easygoing, and gentle.

I first met Charlie three days before my solo 1988 trek. The local Inuit were concerned about my safety because I would be traveling among polar bears. They offered me one of their best bear dogs as a gift, but I insisted on paying one hundred dollars for him, all I had left in my expedition budget. As soon as I saw the big, nameless dog, I fell in love with his soft eyes and tenderness. I called him Charlie, and we set forth together to the Pole. We bonded and became best friends. Along the 364-mile journey he protected me from seven polar bears and even saved my life when one charged me.

I'll never forget that experience. As we approached an area of extremely rough ice, frequented by numerous bears, Charlie suddenly stopped and refused to follow me around a thirty-foot-high mound of ice. Instead he growled a warning. I stopped, released my sled harness and skis, and waited with a pounding heart. Moments later, an enormous male bear stepped out from behind the ice and paused, then charged straight to my 160-pound sled and flipped it over as if it were a toothpick.

Next, fixing his eyes on me, he gathered his powerful body and prepared to charge. With a speed born of terror, I unclipped a release on Charlie's collar. Bursting loose with an earsplitting growl, Charlie raced at the bear, grabbed his right rear heel, and hung on. The bear, his attention now turned to Charlie, spun in tight circles, reaching back to grab his tormentor. But Charlie evaded his grasp and hung on with all his might.

Finally, in desperation, the bear tore loose and raced across the ice with Charlie in hot pursuit, no doubt enjoying the most wonderful bear chase of his life. I watched them disappear, astonished to have survived. Thirty minutes later Charlie trotted back. I ran to greet him with a grateful hug. Then he received his reward: peanut butter cups. He'd found them on my sled earlier in the expedition, and they'd become his favorite food.

Bill and I hoped Charlie would be the key to our studies of wolves this summer and winter. We had many uncertainties, and everything depended on the wolves' acceptance of Charlie as a go-between.

After my second ski trek to the magnetic North Pole, this time with Bill in 1992, we flew back to our base camp at Resolute Bay in the Canadian Arctic. There we met Ian Randle, a noted British biologist who had come there from England to study arctic gray wolves. Over dinner at Resolute Bay, Ian agreed that our plan might work. "It's extremely difficult to study wolves in the wild," he told us. "They're smart, cautious, and hard to see. But if you're persistent, you have a good chance with Charlie as your alpha. I know of dogs and wolves who respect each other. Your situation is unique. Charlie's genes and experience could lead you to success."

Having resolved to take Charlie with us, our next question was where we could find wolves. We were fairly sure we knew of a good winter location—the Mackenzie River Delta close to Inuvik in the Northwest Territories, not far from Canada's northern coast. An Inuk friend had told us he had located and watched a group of wolves there during several winters.

Choosing the summer location was more difficult. Considering our many years of Arctic experience, one of the Arctic islands with unlimited visibility across the treeless tundra at first seemed logical. But our thoughts soon moved south to the tundra and mountains of the Canadian Yukon Territory, which we had also explored many times.

The northern Yukon is an immense, mostly uninhabited space, one of the world's last great wildernesses. Vast expanses of flat and rolling tundra silently sweep the spaces between mountain ranges. Here and there, stunted, twisted stands of black spruce struggle to penetrate the permafrost—a continuous layer of frozen earth a few feet to two thousand feet thick—as the roots seek nutrients from the frozen soil. Wildlife abounds and the sun shines twenty-four hours a day in summer. The barren, rocky summits cast long shadows across the land.

As summer slips into winter, the tundra foliage turns a dazzling red, orange, and yellow. Radiant displays of northern lights, or aurora borealis, grace the dark winter heavens. As snow begins to fall, the tundra's tiny plants, some of which grow only a few inches in a hundred years, become dormant. The land's many moods, its challenges, and most of all its peace, continue to attract us.

Although the difficult terrain could make our already daunting task even more of a struggle, the Yukon might be the perfect place, especially if we found a relatively inaccessible area where hunters rarely visited. Wolves might be less cautious around us if they had not already been habituated to humans.

We flew home from Resolute Bay having decided to make a reconnaissance trek with Charlie to the Yukon's Richardson Mountains. If we found wolves and if Charlie could communicate with them successfully, as he had in the Arctic, we would have an indication that the plan might work, and we would begin preparing for an expedition the following summer. We realized there was a serious possibility that they might not accept Charlie or, worse, might attempt to kill him. But we reasoned that if he remained on his leash at all times he would be safe. He would always be close to Bill and me, and we would have complete control over how closely he could approach wolves. (We were never concerned that the wolves might attack us.

Normally, wolves prefer to keep their distance from humans—
and as we would learn later, with good reason.)

🐾

Now, after eight weeks of searching and disappointments, we
had found a den. The mountains and ridges surrounding this
remote valley of open tundra would provide good views of the
wolves as they carried out their daily routines and traveled back
and forth from their hunts. And Charlie's successful conversation with the wolves was a hopeful sign that they would allow us
to camp near their den next summer.

That night we jubilantly celebrated our success and Charlie's
first wolf contact. We broke out the macaroni and cheese and
opened a bottle of apple cider we had brought for just this occasion. As we raised our camp mugs under the sun-filled summer
night sky, Bill exclaimed, "A toast to the wolves and Charlie!"

Trekking across the tundra and into the mountains with Charlie, who I
hope will facilitate our contact with the wolves.

Summer

Approach

I N APRIL, nine months after our reconnaissance trip, Bill, Charlie, and I returned to the northern Yukon to begin our adventure among the wolves. First, though, we needed to buy a few final food provisions to add to the six months of food, gear, and stove fuel we had already stockpiled. We'd have the help of Margaret Leyland, an energetic New Zealand outdoorswoman whom we'd chosen to be in charge of our resupplies because of her gift for handling the logistical details of an expedition.

All four of us, and our packs and gear, squeezed into Margaret's pickup truck for the drive from our home near Seattle to Dawson City, a town located on the far western edge of the Yukon and made legendary during the Klondike gold rush days. The 2,000-mile journey took a mere four days, in contrast to the many weeks it required of the prospectors.

When we piled out of the truck in Dawson City, were it not for the many tourists snapping photos, we almost thought we'd stepped back in time. The rickety grocery store where we bought a few last necessities had uneven wooden floors, and many other buildings seemed to have jumped right out of a history book, from Diamond Tooth Gertie's Gambling Hall to the Red Feather Saloon.

Now a town of just a thousand people, Dawson City enjoyed its heyday back in the 1890s, after three crusty Alaskans, George Carmack, Tagish Charley, and Skookum Jim, stumbled across dime-size gold nuggets in the bottom of a remote stream. Others had passed over the wild area in favor of more inviting places, never dreaming of the riches in that shallow water. News of the find spread rapidly to the outside world, and soon thousands of men and women began one of the biggest stampedes in history.

To get to the goldfields, prospectors traveled over treacherous mountain passes, enduring subzero temperatures and blizzards. They hauled their supplies by hand or by horses, some even using dogs or cattle. After surviving the land portion of the journey, many gold seekers met their death on the churning white-water stretches of the Yukon River. At the height of the gold rush, the population of Dawson City, a trading post built on a mud flat at the confluence of the Klondike and Yukon Rivers, mushroomed to more than 20,000.

By 1900 the rush was over. A few fortunate men went home rich, but most, due to poor luck, gambling, and other hardships, returned without the wealth they had sought. Now all that remains is a picturesque ghost town: potholed streets, weathered buildings, unsightly piles of rocks left by the gold-mining dredges. Robert Service, the famous poet, once lived in a rustic cabin on the hill at the back of town. Here he wrote some of his best poetry, such as "The Shooting of Dan Magrew."

As the snow melted in the early spring thaw, we hurried around town gathering the last of our supplies, dodging raindrops and jumping across rapidly expanding mud puddles. We hoped to leave before dark, but Dawson City is not a place where you rush anything. After the first few curious stares, we slowed our pace to become less conspicuous.

By late afternoon we still had not completed our to-do list, so we took a room at a bed-and-breakfast for the night, after receiving assurance that Charlie was welcome. The floors creaked with every step, and the furniture was worn from many years of visitors. But Charlie immediately jumped onto the bed and lay back in complete comfort. When we spread a sleeping bag on the floor, he eyed it ruefully; only after considerable urging from Bill did he consent to leave the bed and sleep on the bag.

The next day we completed our shopping in clear weather. Tourists stopped to pat Charlie and tell him what a fine fellow he was. He relished the attention.

At last our seventy-pound packs were crammed full of gear and supplies, including Charlie's favorite kibble. Over the previous two months Margaret had amassed enough reserves to keep us provisioned during what we hoped would be a six-month stay at the wolf den. With the truck loaded, we were finally poised to begin our adventure.

We were about to enter a world where spring and summer plant growth accelerates unbelievably. As the summer solstice approaches, the sun stays above the horizon twenty-four hours a day, bathing the tundra in continuous light for several weeks. Flowers, sedges, and mosses grow with a frantic vigor to take advantage of the long days, which all too soon are replaced by darkness and cold. Ahead of us lay a wilderness, natural and free from humans, without the bustle of regulated national parks or the trappings of interpretive centers. Animals rule as they have for hundreds of millennia. The greens, browns, reds, and yellows of plants and trees blend with the stark gray mountains as if swept by a giant stroke of a heavenly artist's brush.

Under sunny skies we traveled the Dempster Highway across the Yukon Territory, as we had done on our reconnaissance journey the year before. This potholed, tire-eating "highway," which was completed in 1979 to exploit the oil reserves of the far north, winds through subarctic wilderness and ends in the modern town of Inuvik, about 475 miles northeast of Dawson City. Apart from scattered basic campgrounds and a few native communities, there are few vestiges of human presence along the road's length.

Our first stop was Eagle Plains, 254 miles from Dawson City and only five miles as the crow flies from the Arctic Circle. The settlement, built on a plateau more than a thousand feet high, has 360-degree views. The town takes its name from the nearby river and consists of a hotel, a few small buildings, some fuel tanks, and a gas station that does a brisk business repairing flat tires and selling new ones to replace those shredded by the sharp shale that covers most of the highway.

After Eagle Plains, the road stretched for miles northeast across the treeless tundra to the distant gray slopes and smooth summits of the Richardson Mountains. The wide-open tundra was breathtaking in its expanse. Its magnitude reduced living things to mere specks. To some this seemingly empty place would hold no interest, but to me it radiated a wild pulse. In these enormous reaches I felt a new excitement as I took in the stark beauty of a land that for centuries had remained unchanged and had no boundaries. A sense of well-being coursed through my body. At that moment I understood why wild animals must remain wild. These are the places where wolves belong.

After descending the plateau, we drove north across the Arctic Circle, positioned at 66 degrees, 30 minutes north

The vast tundra stretches before us.

latitude. Here on the summer solstice the sun does not set, while on the winter solstice it does not rise.

We then lost more elevation as we crossed the tundra toward the summits and ridges of the Richardson Mountains. They were named after Sir John Richardson, the scientist on Sir John Franklin's expedition of 1819, which set out from England to discover the Northwest Passage.

Approximately ninety miles and one blown-out tire after Eagle Plains, we stopped at a wide, lonely spot, unloaded our packs, and said a cheery "Good-bye, see you later" to Margaret. She headed off, driving north to Fort McPherson, where she would stay in a rented cabin until we were ready to leave the wolf den in October.

Bill and I were eagerly anticipating spending a long summer in the immense solitude of the wilderness, which was even more magnificent than we'd remembered. Great bare summits reached skyward all about us, with rivers and streams cascading down their rocky faces. Liberated from the world we had left behind, we were free to follow our dreams. Charlie tugged at his leash to urge us on, and Bill enthusiastically punched his fist skyward. We were off!

We set out on a different route from the one we had traveled during our reconnaissance trek; the nine-day hike would allow for a direct but still cautious approach to the den site. Happily, despite our relatively diminutive frames—Bill's five feet five inches and my five feet two—we easily managed carrying our heavy packs over the rugged, often steep mountain terrain day after day. At sixty-nine and fifty-eight, respectively, Bill and I kept ourselves in excellent physical condition through extensive weight training in our home gymnasium, a dedicated running program, and hundreds of miles of challenging mountain hikes. And now, every breath of mountain-scented air made the weight of my pack feel even lighter.

Our journey began with Bill taking Charlie's sturdy but lightweight nylon hiking leash and leading the way. After several stops to make sure I was following close behind, Charlie let us know that he wanted me to take his leash, at least for now. Although he was also bonded to Bill, many times when we hiked in unfamiliar territory Charlie would signal that he wanted me to take his leash, until he was sure of where we were and what was expected of him. "Charlie's telling me he needs his mother," Bill would laugh on such occasions.

With Charlie in the lead we trekked over a five-hundred-foot pass, then followed a shallow stream into the shadows. Misshapen spruce, ancient dwarf willow, and barely visible cotton grass covered the snow-dappled valley floor. As the late-afternoon sun dropped beyond the mountains, the way ahead led through tall willow thickets, sparse taiga forest, and melting snow. It took little to persuade us to make camp in the shadows of the trees and tackle the tangled brush the next morning.

Birds chirping from the nearby forest canopy awoke us just as dawn's soft light arrived. Charlie stretched and yawned. He had slept well—not surprising considering that he had taken up a large portion of my bed for most of the night. Around midnight, I had felt his generous frame overflow across my bag, giving me only half the length I needed. Too groggy to argue, I had turned over, shifting into the shape of a pretzel to accommodate him. But I made a mental note that things would have to change.

Now, though, a refreshed Charlie was ready for breakfast. I slowly unwound my body and adjusted the kink in my back. "Charlie, you have to stay on your own pad from now on," I said irritably. "My back is killing me."

Bill, still snuggled deep in his bag, laughed. "You might as well save your breath. He's not going to move, and you're never going to make him move."

"Well, you tell him to move."

"Never," came the muffled reply. Charlie had won again.

It was my turn to get breakfast for the team. With my hand on the tent zipper, ready to make as graceful an exit as my aching back would allow, I suddenly froze as a rustling sound came from the direction of the spruce trees. Charlie growled. Moments later, a nearby metallic crash shattered the peace of the early-morning forest. Charlie's warning grew louder as he snarled, straining at the end of his sturdy leash, trying to get through the door to what we guessed was a bear rummaging through our camp. The animal was attacking our cooking gear with gusto. By the sounds of the racket, he was dramatically shortening the useful life of our pots and pans.

Bill, who had sat up in bed at Charlie's first warning, now had his shotgun in hand. Cautiously he unzipped the main tent door while I opened the back. I looked out and immediately retreated in horror. I was inches from the brown, furry side of a large, angry grizzly.

Without seeing me, he bounded around to the front of the tent. With the barrel barely clearing the doorway, Bill fired a shot into the air. The earsplitting boom at first had no effect, but after another deafening warning blast, the bear loped a few yards into the taiga forest. Then he turned to face us, defiantly rising high on his rear legs to get a better view. After a short pause, he dropped to all fours and lumbered away.

With Charlie at our side, we clambered out of the tent and stood listening for the possible return of our uninvited guest. Every sound was magnified in the heavy silence. Charlie never took his eyes away from the direction in which the bear had headed. Staring into the dim forest light, we could imagine the bear watching us. But as the first warming rays of sunlight peeked over the ridge, we saw no more sign of him.

Our food cache, which we had strung high in a neighboring tree, was still intact. We gathered our stove and pots and pans. Apart from a few dents, everything was still usable. We chose to eat a cold breakfast instead of cooking, to avoid producing mouthwatering odors a passing bear couldn't resist. Charlie gobbled his kibble, still edgy, which made us wonder just how far the bear had gone. At one point he looked up from his breakfast with a quiet growl, searching the woods as though his keen ears had picked up a sound beyond our hearing. Several minutes later he resumed eating, apparently satisfied that no danger lurked in the shadows.

As the sun climbed higher, spreading its long fingers of golden light across mountaintops still blanketed in snow, we loaded our packs and heaved them onto our backs. The bear episode inspired us to leave early.

Bill led the way while Charlie and I followed. Dogs and grizzlies by reputation do not get along. We kept Charlie on a short leash, although we knew he would welcome another grizzly appearance, another opportunity to protect us from harm and possibly get to chase a bear. He had warned me of polar bears on the ice cap, and now he was alert and ready to warn us as we traveled through grizzly country in the Yukon.

Our first challenge that day was a dense willow thicket. Our packs tangled with the protruding branches, and our bootlaces straggled loose. Charlie fought his way through the dense undergrowth. As Bill trailblazed, he described the entire area in rather graphic terms while I mumbled something about our poor choice of route. Dew soaked our shirts and pants, adding to our misery. By the time we cleared the entanglement, we looked as though we had walked through a rainstorm. We were drenched and our tempers were frayed. Only Charlie was in good spirits. He shook the water from his thick black coat, showering our already dripping clothes.

I pulled the clammy fabric of my shirt away from my body as I looked ahead, hoping to detect an open route. But all I could see was more willows. "This stuff is enough to make me wish I had never left home," I grumbled.

"It can't get worse," Bill said, adjusting his pack over his wet shirt. "Maybe after we clear this next mess of willows, it'll get easier. If it doesn't ease up soon, we'll have to take to the ridges."

Charlie was the only one with the right attitude. With a gentle wave of his tail, he tossed his head back and gave a high-pitched bark. A sharp tug on his leash relayed the message that he was ready to travel whether we were or not. Rather than change into dry clothes, we decided to follow and allow the warm sun to dry us. Happily, our luck changed; as soon as we cleared the thicket and rounded a few spruce trees, we were greeted by the sight of open tundra.

Even though we had to cross areas of soft snow, the footing was solid enough to allow faster hiking compared to our slow start. As we warmed up, our good humor gradually returned. It was lunchtime when we entered a thicket of untidy spruce that soon thinned to an orderly forest of twenty-foot-high trees. Bill noticed a low rocky knoll sheltered by a few shade trees, a perfect lunch spot. Gratefully, we lowered our packs from tired, sweaty shoulders.

Charlie stretched out full length for his noon nap while we took out a bag of nuts and dried fruit. Two trees made excellent backrests for us, adding to our comfort. But just as we were congratulating ourselves on choosing such a fine site, the sharp crack of snapping twigs in the forest straight ahead interrupted our tranquility.

In an instant, Charlie was awake and on his feet, staring in the direction of the sound. All at once, a playful young grizzly galloped out of the trees. The large form of another bear, probably his mother, remained in the shadows. The youngster, perhaps a year and a half old and only two hundred yards away, picked up a large stick, chewed it, then tossed it in the air. Charlie, sensing there was no danger, sat on his haunches and watched quietly.

We were downwind and shielded by trees. Not daring to move lest we attract the bears' attention, we at first sat motionless. Then I slowly lifted my camera from its resting place at my side and discreetly photographed the young grizzly as he played. Meanwhile, just in case, Bill reached for his shotgun, which he carried lashed to his pack.

As we watched, fascinated, the little bear found a larger stick and proceeded to strip the coarse brown bark from its surface until the wood disintegrated. Then he wandered into the stream and caught a small fish, but soon lost interest and dropped it. Splashing his way out onto the low streambank, he gave a gigantic shake and then rolled in the grass to dry, just as piglike grunts came from deep in the forest. The young bear paused, then loped obediently back to his mother, his healthy coat rippling across his shoulders as he moved. Mother and son vanished into the trees.

Charlie stood, stretched, and lay down to finish his nap. Bill and I leaned against our two trees and began to breathe again, still incredulous that we had witnessed a grizzly bear at play. "The right place at the right time," I said.

"I wonder where they'll sleep tonight," Bill said.

"In a safe place but away from our camp, I hope."

After a brief rest we set out again, stopping only when the mountain shadows once more reached across the valley. We stored our food bags as high as possible in a convenient spruce tree. After dinner we slid into our sleeping bags and dropped promptly off to sleep.

About midnight, Charlie woke us by jumping to his feet. Ears forward, alert, he was listening to something outside. Bill and I sat up, mirroring Charlie's silence. Then, with ears tuned to the slightest sound, we eased out of our sleeping bags. Bill again reached for the shotgun. Outside, we could hear paws crossing the mossy ground.

Bill whispered, "Watch the back door. I'll go to the front."
We heard a quiet grunt followed by a yip. From the opposite side
of the tent came an answering yip.

Wolves! Now we understood Charlie's absolute quiet. He
knew that wolves had surrounded the tent, and although he was
used to wolves in the Arctic, he chose a respectful silence
around these strangers.

More soft, careful footsteps circled us, followed by loud
sniffing at the base of the front door, only inches from Bill's
crouched, tense body. Probably one of our visitors was trying to
discover the contents of our home.

Soon the footsteps faded. Charlie slowly relaxed, then lay
down, still alert, on my now empty sleeping bag. Eager to investigate, we stepped outside. A full moon glowed in the starry sky,
lighting the night and casting long shadows across the nearby
spruce forest.

Deep within the woods, a great hoot pierced the stillness.
Then came an answering hoot, followed by quiet. I wondered
what these owls were saying
to each other.

Charlie senses wolves close by.

As Bill and I started
back to the tent, a long,
richly toned howl surged
from the shadows, followed
by a higher-pitched howl
joined by several other
voices. We spun to face the
trees as the eerie chorus car-
ried through the treetops and faded away, only to start all over
again with another great howl.

Chills coursed down my spine. At the first howl, Charlie
instinctively went to our side. As the howls subsided, he sent a
soft *woof* in reply. We strained to see, but we could only imagine
what was out there. A sudden loud hoot from an owl made my

heart race, while Bill visibly jumped. Only Charlie was unperturbed. He wandered off to the tent to once more claim most of my sleeping bag.

Bill and I watched and listened until we began to shiver, then reluctantly returned to the tent, too excited to sleep. We were reasonably sure these wolves were from the pack we had seen at their den the year before, and we assumed they were checking us out as we entered their territory.

At first light we discovered the wide paw prints of wolves in the soft snow. The tracks surrounded our tent and led away to follow a well-worn trail that disappeared into a shaded ravine. After Charlie sniffed the tracks he eagerly marked his territory, just as we guessed our wolf visitors had marked theirs during the night. We marveled at his copious supply of urine as he went about the serious business of placing boundaries until he achieved satisfaction. Only then did he turn his attention to breakfast.

Our lack of sleep left us yawning and listless. Just as I wondered aloud if we might take the liberty of sleeping two hours past dawn before starting the day's trek, I saw movement on a low ridge to the west.

A lone black wolf was watching us. Minutes later, four others crested the hill, standing as still as stone statues in shafts of sunlight.

"We've still got visitors," I said.

"No more sleep," Bill said with resignation. "We'd better get going." Although there was no danger of an attack, we knew we could be interrupting the pack's routine. Their intense surveillance might indicate that we were close to their hunting trails. The wolves continued to watch from the ridge as we broke camp. Now and then other wolves joined the five, stayed awhile, then left.

Charlie surveyed them with casual interest and then returned to eating. He appeared to regard the pack as friends, as he had the arctic wolves. His calm reactions bolstered our hope that when we reached the den he would be able to communicate with the wolves, winning their trust and enabling us to camp near enough to the den to observe wolf behavior at close range.

We set a lively pace along a foot-wide game trail that led us east, away from the wolves. We crossed packed snow that received little sun as we traversed the foothills of the 3,000-foot peaks closely bordering our route.

A half hour later, Bill stopped. "I feel like we're being watched," he said, looking puzzled.

I'd had the same feeling ever since we left camp. "Let's just keep walking and see what happens," I said. "Maybe it's our imagination."

Charlie also seemed to sense something. Now and then he paused to raise his nose, as if checking a wild scent drifting by. A hundred feet farther along the trail, he stopped and looked into the trees.

We listened but heard nothing. Reasoning that Charlie would warn us of an approaching bear, I suggested that we step up the pace and try to outdistance whatever was following us. A short tug on Charlie's leash sent him to his usual position in front.

Minutes later, wolves appeared in the thick willow undergrowth and spruce trees, silently surrounding us. A large black male stood calmly observing us with his amber gaze. He blocked our path.

An urgent "Here, Charlie" brought our companion close to my side. As he returned the stranger's stare he stood tall, tail curled high to display his alpha status, ears forward, without animosity or submission. An understanding seemed to pass between Charlie and the wolf. Then the black stranger turned his lean body and, in a blur, disappeared to join the other wolves, who had remained in the shadows.

Charlie whipped around to face the rear. We followed his gaze but could see and hear nothing. Turning his attention once more to the trail ahead, he pulled to tell us it was time to leave. The wolves had left as silently as they had arrived, but for the next half hour we couldn't rid ourselves of the sense that we were being followed.

We camped on snow in the deep sunless valley and spent the next day climbing over 2,000-foot naked summits. The following day we traversed precarious caribou trails that clung to the steep mountainsides. On the narrow crest of a rocky ridge, Charlie tensed as he spied two wolves below. After a concentrated stare, he sent a long howl of varying notes to the distant figures. Just before trotting single file into a thicket of dwarfed trees, one of the pair answered with a long, low howl. Charlie echoed them but, receiving no answer, resumed his journey.

We were elated that Charlie had received an answering howl so soon in our trek. The wolves hadn't panicked or shown any sign of nervousness, even though we were closing in on their den.

As we traversed yet another narrow, precipitous caribou trail that continually broke away beneath our boots, Charlie leaped from one rock to another, skillful as a ballet dancer. Bill and I, under the weight of our backpacks, were far less light-footed. When the trail gave way, we slid downward with flailing arms for several feet, in an avalanche of small rocks. At each ridge top we hoped to see an end to our ordeal, but instead we saw only more steep slopes of barren gray, rocky trails, some even more exposed than those we had already crossed. A wrong step could send us hurtling several hundred feet downward. Our heavy packs would make it impossible to stop a slide and could even cause us to tumble head over heels.

Bill was usually stoic in hazardous mountain conditions, but the rocky terrain tested even his patience. "Is this blasted stuff going to last forever?" he muttered.

I felt even less charitable. We stopped to assess the route ahead, hoping to see an easier, safer path, but there seemed to be no way around the dangerous slopes. We crossed each slope one at a time to avoid the possibility of both of us being caught in the same avalanche of falling rocks. When it was my turn I became the nervous mother, keeping a white-knuckled grip on Charlie's leash in case he slipped.

But Charlie's calm stride reminded me that he was far more sure-footed than I. In truth, I was only adding to his danger by holding his leash in such a death grip that if I fell, I would drag him downward with me. After crossing the first slope, I let him off the leash. He immediately bounded across the next slope ahead of Bill and stood patiently waiting for me to follow.

After one more troublesome day of precipitous slopes we descended the eastern mountains to enter easier terrain in a world of black spruce, willows, native grasses, and sedges. Tiny surprises grew in the crevices: Persistent early-season wildflowers thrust their showy heads upward to meet the light. Bogs of green and brown moss occasionally blocked our path.

We splashed through knee-deep rivers that, although no more than ten feet wide, quickly numbed our feet and legs. Charlie, disenchanted with swimming, showed his displeasure by attempting to look for a shallow crossing. After I gave him several tugs on his leash and words of encouragement, he agreed to cross with us. The rivers and streams, some no more than a quiet trickle, all drained from the eastern mountain slopes to the Peel River fifty miles away. We passed two miniature glassy lakes separated by a thick patch of black spruce. All around us a springtime explosion of green life thrust itself through melting snow.

After another day spent climbing and scrambling, we camped early beside a foot-wide stream. Even Charlie was tired. Without ceremony he spread out on the soft earth with a contented sigh.

A young grizzly plays with a log while we remain hidden.

The tent was barely erect when a large grizzly walked by, a silent dark shadow, only two hundred yards away, his chocolate-colored fur covering a powerful body. We each grabbed our shotguns, but the bear only glanced in our direction, displaying little interest, and then disappeared into the brush.

Charlie was unconcerned. He raised his head, decided there was no danger, and returned to his dreams.

"How can Charlie sleep at a time like this?" I marveled.

Until we two troubled humans were sure the bear wouldn't return for another look, we kept a nervous watch, but only silence floated on the breeze as Charlie slept on.

Trust

SIX DAYS AFTER LEAVING MARGARET, we neared the wolf den. For most of the morning we crossed bogs, enduring icy water flowing over our boot tops. The afternoon was a forced march through an entanglement of head-high willows. Our mood darkened by the hour as we struggled with maddening thickets that twisted in every direction. One small branch jabbed Bill's left eye, drawing blood, which caused our fast-diminishing good spirits to dwindle even further.

It wasn't fun for Charlie either. At one point he sat down and refused to move. His body language firmly informed us that he had had enough and was going on strike. We sat with him, offering tidbits of beef jerky and other tasty morsels. But when we attempted to resume our hike, Charlie only sat and begged for more treats. Only after another half hour of shameless begging and snacking did he finally agree to accompany us.

We crawled on hands and knees through branches that snagged our packs, then changed tactics and, in desperation, tried a stand-up charge. But the more aggressive strategy made no difference. The wall of branches dictated our dismally slow pace. With our sleeves pulled down, collars pulled up, and gloves pulled on, we did everything we could to minimize the punishment to our bodies. Finally, at 5 P.M., an inviting clearing lay just one hundred feet ahead. Our ordeal was over.

As we broke clear, Charlie's tail fanned back and forth; he seemed relieved too. We set up camp in a miniature, snow-free meadow tucked into a gap at the base of a rock cliff. A cup of hot chocolate restored our optimistic mood, although we both agreed that if we encountered more dense undergrowth, we would go miles out of our way rather than bushwhack again.

Charlie rose at four the next morning, eager to go outside. His breakfast normally took top priority, but a scent out there preoccupied him today. He raised his sensitive nose in the brisk breeze. After catching just the right whiff, he let loose with a long, wild howl that spiraled down the scale to resonate off the mountainsides all around us. Immediately, an answering far-off cry drifted back to us, followed by additional voices with different pitches. We were ecstatic.

Because a pack's hunting territory ranges over many square miles, we were sure the howls were those of our target family. Charlie was already in conversation with them. To allow the wolves time to accept our approach to their den, we would now change tactics and begin a slow, nonthreatening advance to gain their trust.

Charlie, two days from the den.

Under sunny skies, we broke camp and descended into a short valley, skirting willow thickets as we went. Preoccupied with wolf scent, Charlie stopped frequently, at times cocking his head to one side. He occasionally paused to howl, then listened for a reply. Once in a while wolf voices, which drew closer as the day wore on, answered him. Here and there a scent attracted Charlie's attention. He followed with his nose close to the ground, at the end of his leash, pulling us along.

Around noon, just as we veered around a rock incline, the appearance of two wolves startled us. Both stood motionless, watching from an outcrop a hundred feet away. One was the same black wolf we had seen earlier; the other was gray.

Charlie stopped. For a few moments he calmly returned their steady gaze, then quietly lay in a submissive pose, head resting on his paws and half turned away.

Following his lead, we sat and looked to the side. The two stone-still wolves continued their inquiring stare while we waited for their next move. Ten minutes later, without a sound, they turned and disappeared in the direction of the den.

Charlie stood and pulled on his leash, eager to follow the two scouts. He led us at a rapid pace, ignoring our appeals to slow down. After we scaled a slippery snow-covered rampart, we stopped for the day. The only suitable campsite was a ledge with a narrow flat place barely large enough for our tent.

As we ate a dinner of rice and beans, we planned our approach tactics. Just as mountain shadows plunged us into deep shade, we caught a brief glimpse of a wolf on an exposed ridge three hundred feet to the south. An hour later, another wolf stood watching. The surveillance crew was taking turns keeping an eye on us! Bill and I agreed that they might be getting nervous as we closed in on their den. We would move slowly tomorrow so as not to spook them.

The next morning, after trekking for an hour, we climbed a gradual ridge located a half mile from the den. With powerful binoculars, we scanned the area.

"I see wolves at the den," I said as my heart beat faster. We could be sure of it now: The wolves were using the same den as the year before.

Two wolves lay on a barren patch of earth, stretched out side by side in the sun. Close by, the black and gray wolves we had seen earlier sprawled near huge rocks, enjoying their shade. A blond wolf appeared at the place our memories told us the den entrance should be. Two more wolves, probably lookouts, stood on the highest point around, directly above the den. As we remembered from our reconnaissance journey, the den itself was dug into the side of the steep slope and shielded by boulders.

Suddenly one of the wolves gave a sharp bark. He and his companion must have caught our scent. They bounded down the steep slope to the black wolf's side. All three wheeled to stare directly at us in our exposed position. The two wolves lounging in the sun jumped to their feet to follow their companion's gaze and barked another alarm. Our plans for an inconspicuous approach rapidly crumbled. One wolf returned to the ridge top to continue his lookout duties.

As we watched the wolves, we saw that they had become agitated. We agreed to stop for the day to allow them time to calm down before we moved on. If we approached too quickly, the family might panic.

Out of sight of the den, we camped on a barren gravel patch screened by willows and a few scraggly spruce trees. "We'd better avoid any eye contact," Bill advised. "They might interpret it as threatening." And that, we knew, could cause the entire wolf family to leave the area.

Charlie, unhappy with our choice of a site, pulled at his leash. He wanted to camp where he could see the wolves. Finally he sat down but, moments later, not to be defeated, he tossed his head back and howled to the heavens. A minute later, an answering short call bounded across the valley. Still on his leash, Charlie contentedly returned to the tent and his food bowl. We hoped a friendship had begun.

That night, as we sat on a large, flat rock outside our tent eating a leisurely dinner of freeze-dried vegetables and rice, Bill and I discussed our plans. Although pleased with our progress and encouraged by Charlie's reactions, we were worried that if we moved too fast, we could undo our so-far successful approach. The next few days would be critical. We agreed to adopt a slow, cautious pace while keeping a sharp eye out for nervous reactions from the wolves.

We had originally planned to move ahead the next day, but instead we camped on the gravel patch for the next two days. It was the last week of April. We had the waning days of spring, in addition to all of summer and autumn, to interact with the wolves. We felt no need to hurry. Time was on our side.

While we remained close to our tent we caught up on our journal notes and aired out our sleeping bags and clothing. About midafternoon, Charlie sent a single howl across the valley. Hearing no answer, he returned to the tent and went to sleep. Toward evening, he made another call; this time, answering voices of intermingling tones echoed through the valley. I wondered aloud whether the calls were territorial, meant to warn us away.

"I'd rather believe they're welcoming us," Bill said.

"Charlie seems eager to talk to them," I observed. He was standing at attention, alertly listening to the wolves' conversation. Now and then throughout the day he had suddenly looked up, stared into the brush, and then lay down to display submission. Although Bill and I saw no wolves, we knew they were keeping silent vigil close by.

We busied ourselves with washing clothes in a barely adequate stream at the back of our camp. I mended a willow-torn shirt while Bill repaired a pack strap jerked loose by a branch. During these two days the wolves were less secretive, sometimes boldly watching from rock ledges protruding from the steep slopes above us. Usually Charlie merely glanced at them, but he always showed submission when the black one stood guard.

On the third day we slowly moved our tent two hundred yards closer to the den, to a place where the brush thinned. Halfway through the short move, the terrain forced us to drop into a narrow depression out of sight of the den. Charlie abruptly raised his head, looking to his right and then quickly to his left. Wolves had maneuvered around us in the underbrush.

They circled in and out of the brush, eyes fixed on Charlie, who stood stiff-legged, silent, monitoring them.

I felt panic flood in. What if the wolves had turned against Charlie? Could we protect him from so many attackers at once? I stepped between the wolves and Charlie to shield him, then realized the wolves were showing no aggression.

"Let's sit," I whispered to Bill. We sat on the ground on either side of Charlie, looking down to show our submission.

"They must be testing Charlie. I don't think they'll attack him," Bill said. "But we'd better stay on the ground so we don't look like a threat." As we sat with our eyes averted, the rustle of the brush told us the wolves still surrounded us. But Charlie remained calm, as if understanding all.

After thirty minutes the wolves departed, and we heard nothing but the low moan of a rising wind that prowled the ridge tops. Wispy clouds scattered across the blue sky, signaling a weather change.

Charlie sat in the warm sun as the melting snow dripped from the surrounding rock ledges. But Bill and I couldn't share his relaxed attitude. We were worried that the wolves had staged the afternoon's events to persuade us to leave, and that made us nervous. We decided to camp in the depression that night. Now that we had established continuous contact with the pack, we hoped an unhurried appearance would demonstrate that we were no threat.

"I hope we haven't made a mistake by approaching the den too fast," I said as I cooked a dinner of instant potatoes and freeze-dried peas and beans.

"The next few days will tell us if we should stay," Bill said. "If we seem to disturb them too much, it'd be better to leave than to cause stress to the pack."

The next afternoon we shifted camp without interruption to a wide patch of snow among misshapen spruce trees. The scattered cotton grass was already pushing its new stalks upward to meet the spring temperatures in the midforties.

Late the following day, we broke camp to move another hundred feet closer to the den. We watched for any sign that our approach might frighten the wolves into flight. The evening sun sent golden shafts of light through gaps in the gathering clouds. As we reached a clearing big enough for our tent, we unexpectedly came upon a wolf fifty feet away. His streaked blond-black fur glowed as he chewed what appeared to be a hare. With no sign of alarm, his steady yellow-green eyes swept the short distance from Bill and me to Charlie, who stood rigid and perfectly still.

Fascinated, I stepped forward without thinking. Immediately the wolf's mood changed from calm to defensive. He bared his formidable teeth to warn me away from his meal. I froze. Then, hardly daring to breathe, I slowly stepped back a few paces as I looked away to avoid his angry stare. After I made it back to Bill and Charlie, the wolf relaxed.

Charlie abruptly dropped to the ground on his belly with his front legs straight out, his head meekly resting on his paws. Taking our cue from Charlie, Bill and I also crouched, keeping our gaze low and averted. After a few minutes the wolf resumed eating, although he remained cautious. My mistake appeared to have been forgiven.

Minutes later, the black wolf stepped out from the brush, tail curled high, ears forward and alert. Two immature wolves followed, a gray-black and a blond—last year's pups, now teenagers. These two milled about, suspicious and insecure in contrast to the black male, who continued his proud stare. The first wolf stopped eating and stood over his unfinished meal of hare.

The big black male took a few challenging strides toward us, then stopped in a stare-down, his piercing yellow eyes contrasting with his rich black coat. His proud, authoritative attitude and calm posture showed him to be the alpha male who reigned over the entire wolf family. His penetrating gaze seemed to pierce our souls.

Charlie continued to demonstrate submission while Bill and I remained crouched below the wolves' eye level in a nonthreatening position. After a last stern look at us, the alpha, his gaze softening, turned his attention to the passive Charlie. Then, with a slight wave of his tail he turned away from Charlie and walked to the leftover hare meal, picked it up without so much as a by-your-leave to the owner, and trotted toward the den with his three family members following. It was a haughty display of his superior position.

The two younger wolves, still nervous, tossed frequent glances over their shoulders as they followed the adults. Charlie rose to his feet, carefully marking his territory by urinating in a line a few yards in front of Bill and me. Although we were encouraged by Charlie's exchange with the wolves, the all-important question still remained: Would the pack accept Bill and me?

We camped in the wide clearing surrounded by willows and a few spruce trees for one day before cautiously moving closer to the den. Charlie, clipped to his seventy-five-foot camp leash, remained vigilant, watching for the wolves who occasionally visited nearby, their movements muffled as they remained under cover in the trees.

On the sixth day we set up the tent a few yards beyond the screen of scrub trees and thin brush. At first we couldn't see the den entrance, but when a blue-gray wolf stepped behind three-foot high rocks and didn't reappear, we guessed the entrance lay behind the barrier.

A day later we placed our camp two hundred feet closer. We were now under constant surveillance by the wolves, who sometimes paced back and forth with nervous suspicion but not serious alarm. We kept our gaze averted and moved slowly to prevent startling them. Charlie relaxed in the sun and slept, or sat and gazed at the neighbors. He was fully content now that he could see the wolves.

Finally, after nine days of cautious, unhurried maneuvering, it was time to test the wolves. We needed to determine how close they would allow us to approach. We packed our camp and slowly, with eyes averted and Charlie tugging at his leash in the lead, edged closer.

The wolves clustered together to watch. Tension filled the space between us. The alpha male—tail high, ears forward, lips parted in a partial snarl—stepped in front of his family, ready to defend. The rest waited behind him. Suddenly the two youngsters ran from one adult to the other, seeking reassurance. As the adults gave short barks of alarm, the teenagers became even more agitated, puffing their cheeks out as if sending us silent messages with each breath of air.

We were too close. Immediately we stepped back, sat down, and turned our eyes away. Charlie lay with his chin resting on the ground, also looking away from the wolves. After five minutes of submission, we retreated to a narrow moss- and grass-covered meadow a hundred feet from the den. The pack slowly calmed but remained wary. The alpha's neck mane stood erect as he barked gruffly at us. Two wolves ran from the den area, circled behind us, and stood stiff-legged, watching and barking.

A critical limit had been revealed. At one hundred feet, we had breached the comfort zone of the wolves. We sat for an hour with Charlie, quiet and subdued.

The wolves, although still on guard, gradually relaxed. Even the alpha stopped barking and calmed somewhat, although he still stood regarding us with distrust. The two who had circled behind us rejoined the pack.

"Do you think we've gone too far?" I whispered to Bill. "Maybe we should leave and camp down the valley for a few days to let them calm down."

Charlie wonders how long until dinner.

"They seem to be settling down," Bill whispered back, as he cautiously turned to get a better view of the wolves. "At least that big black fellow has stopped barking and snarling."

"Let's put up the tent and see what happens—if we go slowly with no sudden moves, it might work," I said, with little conviction. Our sudden rejection had left us uncertain about what to do next.

We cautiously rose and erected our tent, keeping our eyes averted. Meanwhile, Charlie walked several feet farther away and lay down, this time with his back to the den.

"We'd better copy Charlie and sit awhile. He seems to know more about this than we do," I said.

Together with Charlie, we kept a low profile for another hour. With an occasional careful sideways glance, we checked on the wolves periodically. Tails still curled high over their backs, they watched us with an uncertainty that eventually faded as evening approached.

To avoid startling the wolves we didn't light our noisy stove, instead eating a cold dinner of high-energy food bars. As night approached, the wolves relaxed even more. Some lay down, while others wandered around the den area. A particularly long-legged male stood on a high ridge above the den, looking away from us across the tundra beyond. We hoped he had accepted us and was looking for prey. Even the teenagers were less suspicious; one picked up a stick and teased the other into chasing her to steal it.

Now that the day's tension had passed, tranquility spread across our camp. We paused to breathe in the fresh scent of spruce trees and admire the lonely splendor of the mountains and ridges surrounding our tiny meadow.

I reached for Bill's willow-scarred hand and whispered, not wanting to break the peaceful spell, "I think we've made it."

He squeezed my hand and whispered back, "Yes, thanks to Charlie."

Charlie, outside on his long camp leash, gobbled his dinner in his usual haste, his appetite unaffected by the excitement. Next he marked his territory by lifting his leg every few yards. To complete his territorial circle, he sniffed a few of the marks he had made, then vigorously scratched dirt in a few places around the circle. Now he walked over to the tent and, before we could stop him, urinated on the side closest to the den to leave his scent. In seconds the sharp aroma of urine had begun to infuse our wilderness bedroom.

With that, he stepped inside the tent, gave a contented sigh, and settled himself down, apparently well satisfied with his day's work. We knew it was all part of claiming his territory, and gave our own sighs as all three of us headed off to dreamland.

Camp

THAT FIRST NIGHT, our excitement allowed us to sleep only a few hours. The next morning, as dawn brightened into day, we awoke and cautiously looked outside. We saw only two wolves, who soon left, following a path that disappeared into the nearby trees. The ensuing silence made us wonder if the entire family had abandoned the area while we slept.

Charlie ate his breakfast with no apparent concern about our neighbors, but Bill and I were too nervous to eat. Our main concern wasn't that we might be attacked, but that the wolves would abandon the den. We kept watch, hoping they would return. Although by midmorning we still saw no wolves, Charlie's continued relaxed posture gave us hope.

Around noon the wolves drifted back, carrying two hares and part of a Dall sheep. We were relieved to see that they were continuing to hunt and bring food back to the den despite our presence. It was a sign that we hadn't disrupted the rhythm of their lives.

Although the family lived in a remote, rugged area deep in the mountains, they had an unobstructed view of the nearby ridges and the game trails. Several well-worn trails led from the den through the nearby forest and valleys, indicating that this was a popular site that had been used for many generations.

We guessed that the den's narrow entrance opened into a wider living space farther back in the slope. From the summit, the pack spent many hours watching for prey across the almost treeless tundra and the distant muskeg, an ancient wetland of peat and low plants. A shallow stream nearby provided constant water. Several dugouts had been excavated in the rocky slopes, beneath overhangs that offered shelter from the sun and rain. Water, the concealed den area, and the surrounding terrain perfectly suited the secretive nature of wolves in the wild.

Wolf Camp One, a name that naturally evolved as the weeks went by, would be our home for our entire stay with the wolves. The meadow, softened by native grasses and mosses, lay nestled between the den ridge and another ridge, three hundred feet high and peppered with a few twisted spruce trees. We pitched our tent in the meadow, where we had a clear view of both the den entrance and the main trail leading into the taiga forest. We could also clearly observe the wolves' lookout. The region sloped gently toward the nearby stream that wound through the meadow.

We intentionally situated our tent a few feet lower in elevation than the wolf den so the wolves would be able to look down on us. In our past observations of wild animals, we had always been more successful when they lived above us, a position they regarded as more secure when dealing with humans.

Charlie's long leash allowed him access to all parts of the meadow and reached to within twenty-five feet of the wolf den. In order to ensure his safety, and to prevent him from yielding to the temptation to get closer, we always kept him tethered.

He confidently set about scent-marking to indicate his territory, an area that resembled an irregular circle, with the tent in the center and the stream flowing along one side. Downstream Charlie also lifted his leg at the edge of a brushy area. Although his leash reached beyond his marks another twenty-five feet toward the den, he showed no desire to claim more of that area.

We assumed he had reached some agreement with the wolves over land claims, since there was no challenge from them. While in camp, Bill and I kept to our side of Charlie's marks, especially in the area closest to the den. We wanted to reinforce what we hoped was the wolves' impression that we were Charlie's pack and he was our undisputed alpha male.

After our camp was established, we took some time to simply enjoy the peaceful solitude of the place. I felt liberated, even though we were surrounded by great bare summits that breasted the distant reaches of sky. The clean air and nearby scented woods sprinkled with bird song made life here seem perfect. Beyond our valley and spruce forest, the way widened to tundra, where sparkling streams flowed through sedges and arctic grasses.

While at Wolf Camp One, our goal was to have no impact on the environment. Rather than cutting trees, willows, or other vegetation for fuel, we cooked on a camp stove that used white gas. To safeguard the stream, we never used soap to wash our clothes or utensils; instead we scrubbed the utensils with a coarse pot scrubber and anchored soiled clothing in the stream to allow the water to flow through the fabric for several hours. Throughout the surrounding terrain, we hiked the existing trails rather than cutting new paths.

We dug a five-foot pit for a latrine at the far edge of the meadow, far from the den and stream but still inside Charlie's scent-marked boundary. Worried that the smell might attract wolves, we kept the hole covered with a tightly anchored tarpaulin, but our diligence proved unnecessary. Perhaps out of respect for Charlie, the pack never disturbed the toilet. The scent of Charlie's feces, which we tossed in each day, may have discouraged them from close investigation.

We stored our food in sealed plastic bags to minimize odors that might tempt inquisitive wolves. Because the scent of meat would be too enticing for them, we ate a vegetarian diet of rice, instant potatoes, freeze-dried vegetables, dried fruit, nuts, milk powder, cereals, and peanut butter supplemented with native plants. At the end of our stay we planned to pack out our garbage, fill the latrine, and leave no signs of human habitation.

During the third morning at Wolf Camp One, a low-pressure system that had been threatening the area became a full-fledged thunderstorm. It forced us to seek refuge in our tent, where we listened to the downpour drumming its beat on the tent roof. Lightning struck the ridges; thunderclaps rolled across the mountaintops and tumbled into the valley. The stream swelled to the top of its banks, but didn't threaten the meadow. Two wolves disappeared into the den, but the rest took shelter in the dugouts.

We spent the first few hours of the storm dozing in our warm sleeping bags; then, with the heavy rain still drumming on the tent roof only two feet above our heads, boredom set in. A trip outside to the latrine now and then brought only misery: It was no fun putting on wet raingear and then trying to keep the pelting drops out of the tent as we climbed in and out. By midafternoon Bill was wondering if we should take turns singing. I somewhat unkindly reminded him that his singing voice was even worse than mine and would probably chase all the wolves away forever. Instead we spent the next three hours in a spirited discussion about a future expedition to the Amazon, a place where some torrential rain falls almost every day.

Meanwhile, Charlie contentedly stretched out across my sleeping bag. When I tried to ease him over to Bill's side, he sent me a reproachful look. He normally slept with me, and this expedition was no exception.

By late afternoon the storm had passed, and we emerged from our tent to see the wolves also emerging from their various shelters, one by one, to enjoy the sun that now shone between broken clouds. We were mildly surprised that they did not seem to like the rain, or perhaps it was the accompanying lightning and thunder.

The next day the sun commanded a cloudless sky. As the wet earth dried, the wolves once again stretched out to sun themselves. We aired out our sleeping bags and basked in the sunny meadow, glad to escape the tent's confinement. While we lounged, Charlie energetically refreshed his scent marks. Once satisfied that the job was complete, he stretched out on a mossy patch to sleep.

The first two weeks were a time of adjustment for all. Gradually the wolves relaxed in our presence, but they were not ready to let down their guard. They had accepted Charlie from the beginning; the howls they had exchanged during the days we spent approaching our final campsite now appeared to have been a conversation of testing and then resolution. But during our first two weeks at Wolf Camp One, at least one wolf always watched Bill and me. When either of us moved, sharp eyes followed.

Charlie quickly settled into a routine. His activities alternated between eating, dozing, and watching the wolves. Mealtime was an important affair to Charlie, never to be missed. His favorite resting spots included a particularly soft mossy area by the stream, a grassy mound near the tent, and a smooth spot close to his scent-marked boundaries, which was excellent for observing the wolves' activities. At night, he retreated to his usual place on my sleeping bag.

Now and then he wandered to the stream for a few noisy laps of water, or refreshed his boundaries. These carefully laid markers had been thoroughly inspected by every member of the pack on the first day. Although the borders between the two territories were invisible to Bill and me, clearly Charlie and the wolves understood them.

Our job during this critical time of adaptation was to gain the wolves' trust. We spent considerable time sitting, moving slowly, and feigning disinterest. We dared not climb any of the surrounding ridges that would take us above the level of the den, since that might alarm the wolves. They had to see Bill and me as nonthreatening. Although impatient to be accepted by the family, we tried to remain relaxed and unconcerned deep within, knowing that animals are highly sensitive to emotions.

The first few times Charlie refreshed his scent marks, we trailed a few feet behind him in an attempt to show the watching family that we followed Charlie, not the reverse. When he drank at the creek, we also bent to drink with cupped hands, and only after Charlie had taken his fill. We wanted to demonstrate that we were subservient to Charlie, our leader. As the summer progressed, we became ever more convinced that without Charlie, the cautious family would never have accepted Bill and me. Charlie was our bridge to the wolves.

We counted only seven adults during the first week. The previous year when we had first observed the wolves, there had been sixteen in all, including four pups. The pups were now a year old and almost full-grown. We wondered what had happened to the other two pups and the rest of the group. Mange, parasites, and disease sometimes overtake a pack, but this group appeared to be in excellent health. Perhaps there had been trouble, or maybe some members had dispersed to take up residence elsewhere.

But it seemed unlikely that more than half the group would leave all at once. We doubted that so many could have been hunted and killed from the ground, because of the inaccessibility of the surrounding terrain. Bill's familiarity with aerial hunting led us to fear, uneasily, that humans might be responsible for the reduced numbers.

The remaining wolves displayed a wide range of coat colors: coal-black to blond to gray-blue. Even their eyes were different, including shades of gray, brown, and piercing yellow.

In our journal notes we identified individuals by their color or personality characteristics as we wrote about them. Bill was adamant that we not name the animals or humanize them in any way. I emphatically agreed. To give a wild, noble creature a human name seemed inappropriate. But we found ourselves having to use long, wordy descriptions to identify each wolf, and realized a compromise was in order.

"Perhaps names identifiable with the North might work," I suggested.

Bill agreed and took out the map for ideas. In the end, we named each according to social position in the pack or landmarks on the map, after first determining genders by observing urination postures.

A wolf pack has a well-developed social system that allows it to operate as a cooperative, cohesive unit, giving its members the ability to live together peacefully, hunt successfully, and raise pups. The dominance order is topped by an alpha male and an alpha female. Mature, subordinate animals, or midpack members, are the beta wolves, who share in the food gathering and pup raising. The lowest-ranking wolf is the omega, who is sometimes an outcast and dares to live only on the fringes of family life. The omega is often a beloved member, however; although often the scapegoat, the omega is reduced to the lowest position only because he or she is easily cowed into submission. Normally juveniles do not establish their position until the second year, although as early as a few weeks after birth, the larger pups often begin to show dominance over their smaller siblings.

The black male with almond-shaped, deep yellow eyes had a self-assured, regal presence. He was undisputedly the alpha male, so we called him Alpha. He was striking yet intimidating with his aloof, bold stare. When we had first arrived, it was Alpha who had stood stiff-legged, tail held high, boldly staring at Charlie as if daring him to challenge his authority. But Charlie had displayed the correct submissive posture required for acceptance. After a few days, Alpha's stance and manner toward Charlie had softened.

At first Alpha subjected Bill and me to intense scrutiny. We averted our gaze submissively, but as the days progressed we returned his stare. To look deeply into a wolf's piercing eyes is a stirring experience that demands honesty. Alpha's commanding gaze probed our inner being for signs of weakness or fear. But most of all, he looked for the slightest sign of aggression that might challenge his top position. Happily, after a few weeks, apparently satisfied that we presented no challenge to his authority, Alpha mostly ignored us while he placidly watched Charlie, whom he seemed to deem more worthy of a ruler's interest.

Another large, powerful male was long-legged and elegant, with the gray wolf's typical luxurious gray and blond markings. We named him Denali, after Alaska's most famous national park. Denali did not run, he flowed across the landscape with fluid strides. He later proved to be the hunt leader, even taking over from Alpha when the pack was chasing prey.

We assumed that Denali's superior ability to read prey was the cause of his leadership status. When not hunting, he was a placid fellow who seemed to take everything in stride. At first he displayed the openly curious nature of a typical wolf. He remained cautious and quietly observed us from a distance. When satisfied that we were trustworthy, he turned his attention to Charlie and seldom watched Bill and me.

The two pups from last year were now tireless teenagers. The dark gray one, intense but playful, became Yukon, and her rambunctious blond sister was Klondike, both named after major rivers in the region. Yukon's darker coat, streaked with white, contrasted with Klondike's lighter fur accented with darker guard hairs.

Two weeks later, we named the other three wolves. One was an older blue-gray male with light brown eyes and a graying muzzle. We called him Beta. A gentle soul who led a dignified life, he was the oldest member of the pack and enjoyed a neutral position in the social ranking. Judging by his confident, elegant bearing and the respect shown him by the rest of the wolf family, we guessed that Beta had been the alpha male at one time. Age was probably his conqueror. We could imagine the younger male with a strong personality taking over the alpha role from his elder pack mate.

Changes in pack leadership can be violent affairs that leave a pack in disarray. A large, younger wolf with the alpha characteristics one day discovers that his youthful strength can overcome the pack's reigning leader. Many times there is a fight, and the old leader leaves the pack altogether or steps back in the social order to live a disgruntled existence in his reduced role. Judging from the respect the pack displayed toward Beta, though, we guessed that this particular takeover had been a peaceful, nondisruptive one. Beta showed no animosity due to his changed role, and he appeared to have inherited the job of teaching and disciplining the two teenagers. He was a patient fellow but allowed them to go only so far in their boisterous games and inconsiderate behavior toward others. The teens were more respectful of Beta than of any other wolf, always careful to approach him with eyes cast downward to show submission to his higher rank.

A shy male whose lifestyle was one of submission usually lurked cautiously, alone, on the fringes of the pack. His was the lowest rank in the social order, so we named him Omega. He often watched the antics of the playful teenagers but seldom joined them. Instead he seemed to enjoy playing with the adults. His brown fur was short and wiry, spread over a compact, muscular body. As the scapegoat, Omega usually ate last and was often picked on for no apparent reason. He was even cautious when checking Charlie's scent marks: He would step forward to take a quick sniff, then furtively glance at Charlie as if to make sure he wasn't in trouble for displaying such boldness. Young and healthy, he was normally included in the hunting muster and appeared to accept his role in the social order without malice.

The last one we named was a blond, medium-size female with intense, almond-shaped gray eyes. She had a fiery, strong

Charlie relaxes in his usual place on my sleeping bag.

personality and little patience. We named her Mother because she had swollen nipples, indicating that she had already given birth or was about to. As the alpha female of the pack, Mother sometimes challenged Alpha. She would snatch food from his jaws or even nip him when he was slow to move out of her way. When the hunters brought food back to the den, she was always one of the first to eat.

Alpha appeared eager to please this female and frequently licked her face. We never saw him retaliate against Mother's aggression. The two were a bonded pair. They often slept side by side in the sun. Occasionally Mother joined in a hunt, but more often she lay near the den. She sometimes watched Bill and me with her piercing gray stare that boasted conceit, as if she sought to impress us with her high rank.

The teenagers were almost as large as the adults, but they were still puppy enough to play a variety of games. Their favorite was chase, with tug-of-war a close second. During a game the teenagers would sometimes mistakenly bump into another wolf, who would snarl a warning into the offending teen's face. The chase would stop instantly, only to resume minutes later. Tug-of-war involved what appeared to be the skin of a hare or another small furry animal, probably a leftover from a meal. Only after the skin was completely shredded, and the minute pieces could no longer be grasped in strong jaws, did the game stop. Then both young wolves would flop down, spread out to their full length, and fall asleep soundly.

Denali sometimes joined in the games of chase with the two teenagers, but whenever they offered him a piece of skin to play tug-of-war, he grabbed the skin, and with one powerful jerk of his wide head, the game ended. At other times, when play turned serious and tempers frayed, Beta stepped in. With a few well-placed nips on rumps and shoulders, he brought all activity to a stop. The teenagers would slink away, heads down, knowing they had gone too far. At mealtime they sometimes tried to eat out of turn, which brought Beta's full wrath to bear upon them. Alpha was even stricter when a youngster took food out of turn. Sometimes he grabbed a teen by the neck and pinned her on her back, where she would whimper for forgiveness. The family's strict discipline was impressive.

By mid-May, three weeks after our arrival at Wolf Camp One, we had become a familiar fixture rather than an intrusion. The wolves responded by going about their lives in a less watchful fashion. They still kept a sometimes cautious eye on us, but they did so in an increasingly confident, even somewhat friendly manner. They had no problem with Charlie; it was Bill and I who had to gain their trust. Even the young wolves became more relaxed, engaging in their playful antics as they became accustomed to our presence. This change was encouraging, since the two teenagers had been frantic at the sight of us during our first encounter.

Early morning was often quiet after Denali led most of the pack on a hunt. Usually they left during the night or just before daybreak. At first the teenagers stayed close to the den or wandered about inspecting rocks and the nearby ridge. As the weeks went by, they joined the hunts more frequently.

Charlie quickly settled in. He claimed his property without apology, even to the point of excess. His proud carriage and domineering attitude became more wolflike as he confidently paraded about his territory. Always gentle and affectionate toward us, Charlie always presented himself as our alpha. We were his pack to protect and guide.

Another storm roared across the ridges for two days, but our sheltered valley escaped the full brunt of the raging wind. Usually Alpha, Denali, or Omega, and sometimes all three, stood on the ridge top in the early light, watching for potential prey. But during this bad weather the wolves stayed close to the dugouts and den. Once the sky cleared, they immediately resumed their posts.

Late one evening as we sat writing in our journals, we noticed that the entire family, except Mother, who was inside the den, had gathered about the entrance. All were tense, even the teenagers. They paced about or sat and stared at the den as if expecting something to happen. Charlie stayed close to the boundary nearest the pack, also expectant. After two hours, Alpha, who had remained closest to the entrance, abruptly got to his feet and disappeared inside. A few minutes later he emerged. The family milled about him in happy unison, licking muzzles, wagging tails, and nudging each other's shoulders. Charlie stood too, wagging his tail and yipping. Mother still had not joined the group.

Then it dawned on us: Newborn pups must be the reason for the excitement.

In warmer climates, pups are usually born in April and sometimes in early May, but above the Arctic Circle young arrive later to coincide with warmer weather. After the giddy celebration ended, the wolves relaxed and went back to normal activities—all except Alpha, who remained close to the den entrance. About midnight, he climbed inside and stayed there until daylight.

Charlie returned to the tent and slept soundly by himself on my sleeping bag. Bill and I stayed up all night, determined not to miss a thing. It was a humbling experience for us to witness the family's reaction to the birth of pups. We realized that even though we had been accepted and a bond of reasonable trust had developed, we humans still sat at the edge of wolf life. We could never hope to enter the innermost circle of a family's emotions, yet we were awed by what we witnessed.

We wondered how long it would take for Mother to trust us enough to allow her pups out of the den. Normally they emerge at about three or four weeks; we hoped our presence wouldn't delay the event.

Generally only the alpha male and alpha female, the two highest-ranking wolves in a pack, have pups each year. Often the pair mate for life. Alpha was clearly the father of Mother's pups, but all the wolves helped raise the youngsters. Throughout the summer months, the offspring remained the center of attention for the entire family.

The next day all returned to normal, except that Mother remained out of sight. Alpha and Denali went for a short hunt, and each returned with a hare. Alpha took his catch into the den while Denali gave his to the rest of the pack. Omega stood back and then inched forward, low to the ground, with his tail firmly tucked beneath his body. Just in time he carefully reached forward, grabbed a foot, and trotted off alone to eat. Later Alpha emerged without his hare, which we guessed had been a gift to Mother.

The following morning before dawn, we opened our tent door and looked up to see Alpha, Denali, and Omega standing side by side, completely still, gazing intently into the distance.

Suddenly they bounded down the steep slope to the den, where the pack reverently greeted them with tail wagging and excited yipping. Then Denali and Alpha raced off to the north with Omega and Beta close behind. A hunt was on. They quickly disappeared, leaving us to guess at their prey.

We longed to see a hunt, but bided our time before attempting to follow them. Of course, we realized there would be difficulties. If they traveled far, we could not keep up with their blazing speed and stamina. Perhaps we could camp on a high

place to observe their hunt, or pursue them on one of their shorter jaunts.

At noon all four wolves, with Alpha in the lead, came loping back with food in their jaws. They had killed a moose calf, and their distended bellies showed that they had dined well

Alpha, a strict but benevolent leader.

before heading for home. Alpha took food into the den, while the others dropped their catch on the ground for the rest of the pack. There was so much that Omega ate his fill without having to beg. The teens ate to capacity as well. Then Yukon attempted to carry a leg bone away, but Klondike claimed it as her own.

Just as the battle began, Alpha emerged from the den. With a snarl he nipped Klondike's rear and stood over her as she rolled onto her back, exposing her belly in submission. Yukon picked up the bone and disappeared behind a rock to chew in peace.

After a session of unabashed gorging on the moose carcass, the wolves were too satiated to play. One by one, they lay down in various poses to sleep and perhaps dream of the next hunt. Some moved into the forest, while others sought the shade of a rock overhang. For a time Alpha slept on his back with all four feet pointing skyward. When he changed position he rose to his feet, walked around in tight circles three or four times like a dog, then curled up with his nose tucked under his tail and slept soundly. All was quiet for the next two hours, with only Yukon and Klondike changing to more comfortable positions.

Mosquitoes finally forced the wolves to awaken with cavernous yawns and long stretches. But it was still a lazy time with little to do except relax, swat at the pesky insects, and stare into the distance, with an occasional visit to the creek for a drink. Denali eventually climbed the den ridge to watch for prey, but after a few minutes he relaxed at his watch post and slept. Yukon picked up a piece of moose hide and placed it carefully behind a rock, reserving it to be a toy for a future game, then stretched out again.

Two days later, we saw Mother leave the den briefly. She sniffed the rocks close by, then strolled to the stream to drink. Her belly was less distended, and she looked sleek and healthy. She lay in the sun for an hour before returning to the womblike den. During the first week after the birth, Mother spent most of her time inside, leaving only to relieve herself, drink from the stream, or briefly nap in the sun. The rest of the pack supplied her with food, which Alpha always took to her.

Later, Mother spent increasing time outside sunning and eating food that Alpha and sometimes Denali left for her. Now and then Beta lay alongside Mother and gently licked her face. Mother's personality had mellowed considerably, and she became the object of affection. Even the teenagers took time out from their games to lick Mother and raise a paw to her shoulder or roll over, exposing their underbellies.

The wolves frequently displayed fondness for each other. They played together, shared food, and generally lived a harmonious life. Sometimes they teased a particular wolf, then raced away with the victim in pursuit. They rolled and leaped, raced up and down the ridges, and even played hide and seek.

THREE AMONG THE WOLVES

Occasionally, one wolf brought back a stick and dared another to steal it. When the teenagers broke the rules they were disciplined, sometimes severely, but they were always forgiven.

Charlie's days were busier than ours. After all, he had the responsibility of keeping his boundary marked as well as sniffing scents left by the neighbors. He observed their various games closely, and when a hunting party returned he always stood up to see what they had caught.

Now, in the latter part of May, Charlie no longer presented a submissive posture. He stood tall, with his tail curled above his back, displaying his alpha status. He had gained the confidence of the pack. His dog habits diminished, and his bearing and attitude became more authoritative. He continued his gentle approach with Bill and me, but plainly, he was the alpha and we were his charges.

Often one or two wolves would stroll over to the nearby rocks and, while relaxing in the shade, they would watch Charlie. Their casual postures and gentle facial expressions displayed friendliness. He was at home around them and enjoyed their company. We suspected that the wolves might have invited Charlie to join them at the den. At times he begged to be let off his long leash, but we were afraid to grant his wish. Perhaps we were too cautious, but we could not chance anything when it came to Charlie's safety.

At one point during a particularly energetic game of tug-of-war between Yukon and Klondike, Charlie walked closer, wagging his tail as though asking to join in. The teens stopped and wagged their tails briefly, but gave no sign of invitation. We quietly called Charlie back, and he returned to his favorite mossy spot to watch as the game resumed. We hoped he wasn't too disappointed, and yet we were relieved. We had no intention of allowing Charlie to join the wolves. If trouble developed, we would be unable to defend him.

One night as we slept with Charlie in his usual position on my sleeping bag, a chorus of howls suddenly erupted from the ridge right above us. We crawled outside with Charlie in the lead. Alpha and Beta were facing each other, muzzles lifted skyward. Long mournful sounds flowed from them. The rest of the animals positioned themselves along the ridge. Facing south, led by Alpha, they howled into the summer night. If we had not known how many voices were in this wild chorus, we could have easily estimated many more.

Charlie remained silent, facing south and listening intently as the concert unfolded. Each wolf used a

Mother watches us with suspicion.

different note and volume, creating the impression of large numbers. The notes rose in volume and pitch, then sometimes descended, pausing in the silence, then once more reached a crescendo. At times one or two wolves resorted to yipping notes in odd contrast. The untamed melody unsettled the night. Their voices echoed off the surrounding mountainsides and filled the valley with music from the wild.

The howl of a wolf is perhaps the most unforgettable of all wilderness sounds. Scientists speculate that wolves howl for many reasons. In addition to the sheer joy of a community singalong, they howl to communicate with neighboring packs, to establish dominance over their own hunting range, and to inhibit trespassing by hostile wolves. They often howl immediately before a hunt and sometimes communicate with each other when separated during a long chase. Dispersing loner wolves howl to attract a mate, and packs frequently howl during the breeding season. Howling also emphasizes the messages left on the many urine scent marks on logs, rocks, and trees scattered throughout and along the boundaries of the pack's hunting range. A wolf's ability to increase and decrease volume as it slides its harmonics up and down the scale can cause a listener to assume that there are many more animals in a group than there really are, an advantage if attempting to discourage a threatening pack.

Denali descends the ridge after detecting prey.

The chorus continued for fifteen minutes and then tapered off, with Alpha giving one last mournful final howl that rose to a pitch above all others. The wolves remained on the ridge, still silently watching the southern expanse. Soon a faint howl from a long distance to the south pierced the silence. Each wolf immediately stood and listened intently. In a few minutes the distant howling stopped. Alpha again led a song. After a short silent interval, a single howl quickly joined by many others responded, still from the south.

As the last notes died away, one by one the pack strolled down the ridge to take up restful positions around the den. Mother disappeared inside to tend to the pups. As we listened to the wolves' voices rise from earth to sky, filling this great valley, we understood why North American Indians believed that when wolves howl, they are talking with the spirit world.

Ravens

I T WAS THE LAST WEEK OF MAY. The days had gradually been growing longer ever since we'd set up camp near the den, and now darkness had ceased entirely to fall. We would have twenty-four hours of light for several weeks, making our observation of the wolves easier. Day and night blended together as the pack went about its activities, often hunting in the cooler hours. We occasionally lost track of time and were surprised to find that it was already past midnight. Long days have an invigorating effect on the human body, making it easy to continue working but difficult to keep to a normal schedule. The Inuit of the far northern Arctic often stay up all night during the summer, energized by the sun.

As we watched the wolves' games and family interactions, we could see that they were intelligent animals with the ability to plan and think. Playful by nature, they would carry back to the den various toys such as sticks, stones, animal hides, and bones. Toys not used immediately were carefully placed close by, ready for use later.

The wolves often teased each other into starting a game or taunted a pack mate to get a response. Those in the middle of the pack's social order often harassed Alpha. We noticed, though, that he was always allowed to win the game eventually; no wolf overdid domination when Alpha was involved.

Several ravens lived in the spruce trees and in crevices in the cliffs close to the wolf den. Ravens and wolves are both sociable creatures, and although we would have thought them unlikely companions, they appeared to enjoy each other's company. The ravens liked to tease the wolves and sometimes initiated play with individuals.

While the wolves dozed comfortably one day, a raven appeared as silently as a shadow, landing a few feet from Klondike. It sneaked up behind her, pausing now and then to make sure it had not been detected. When the raven reached the end of Klondike's tail, the bird gave it a quick jab with his large beak, then quickly flew away with a loud squawk and perched atop a six-foot-high rock.

Klondike leaped to her feet in indignation. Seeking revenge, she made futile efforts to scramble up the steep rock. But she slid to the ground each time, her claws leaving long scratches in the rock. Finally the raven flew onto the ridge to await further opportunities. After a few minutes, a disgruntled Klondike resumed her sleep in the protection of a dugout.

Not even Charlie was spared. One day as he lay asleep alongside the stream, two ravens crept up behind him in waddling unison and, as if on cue, both nipped his tail at once. With a loud yelp Charlie jumped up, ready to kill, but the clever birds flew to the ridge where they strutted and cawed, elated at their success. Charlie's indignant bark brought all the wolves to watch and, we supposed, to sympathize as he railed against his tormentors.

One evening when Charlie was engrossed in eating his dinner, three ravens acting as a team swooped down from the cliff. A particularly bold individual led the attack, diving at Charlie's head. When he left his bowl to race after the first bird, the other two made for the abandoned food, stealing as much as they could grab in their large beaks in one low pass. The infuriated Charlie angrily turned and leaped at the ravens, but it was too late. We allowed him to eat inside the tent from then on.

One sunny afternoon Beta rose from a shady spot beside a large rock to stalk a raven who pretended not to notice. As Beta crept closer, the bird hopped ahead, until at the last moment it flew off chattering just as Beta snapped at its tail.

The ravens showed little fear of Bill and me, becoming unbearably bold at times as they strutted and waddled about our campsite with impunity. With heads tipped sideways, they peered at us with their beady black eyes and talked nonstop— about us, we were sure. A few times the birds dived low over our heads, knocking off our caps. They even landed on the tent and pecked the fabric. As a precaution, we kept all our food inside, away from both the wolves and the birds.

At first it puzzled us that the ravens seemed to disappear whenever the wolves were out hunting. One cloudless May morning, hoping to see the wolves leave to hunt, we climbed a nearby ridge that allowed us an unobstructed view of the den area, the valley, and the tundra beyond. Using rocks as back-

rests, we settled down with our binoculars to wait.

An hour later the wolves left the den with their usual exuberant display of tail wagging. As Denali led the hunters through the valley below our ridge, several ravens accompanied them, flying at treetop level.

Klondike at play: A stick will do.

The birds waited on a low branch for the hunters to catch up, then flew ahead, cawing loudly, as if urging the wolves to hurry. Both groups soon crossed the tundra and disappeared into a far valley. If the wolves hunted successfully, we realized, the ravens would also have a feast.

Now we understood why ravens lived close to the den. Not only were the wolves and ravens socially connected, but the wolves also, through their killing of prey, provided food for the ravens. And the ravens didn't just follow the wolves; both species communicated with each other on hunts.

As we continued to observe the two species during the summer, we saw that the information sharing sometimes rose to an even higher level. Twice we watched ravens return to the den and rouse the wolves by flying low and emitting loud squawks. As soon as the birds had gained the wolves' attention, they flew back and forth until the wolves followed them to the source of their excitement: carrion on the forest floor or on the tundra.

On both occasions Alpha, Denali, and Omega followed the ravens while we hurried to catch up. Each time we were quickly left behind, but by taking a shortcut we arrived in time to see both birds and wolves wrestling with the carcasses: a Dall sheep on a slope in the first instance, and a beaver that lay close to a pond in a forest clearing in the second. Both had apparently died of old age or disease. Because of the birds' inability to tear open a tough-skinned carcass, they needed the wolves to do the job for them. The wolves did so, then ate their fill while the ravens, cawing and cackling impatiently, waited close by for their turn. As soon as the wolves departed, the ravens noisily swarmed the carcass. We marveled at these remarkable displays of interdependence and food sharing by two very different wild species.

Ravens, and their smaller cousins the crows, are members of the corvid family. Like wolves, ravens mate for life and can live for twenty years. The birds are intelligent, easily trained, and socially adaptable. They have wingspans of up to four feet with shiny black feathers, a curved, thick black beak, and black feet. At two feet in length from beak to tail, they are the world's largest perching songbirds.

The folklore of the First Nations people of northern Canada contains many legends about Raven that extol the supernatural life of this bird. He is a powerful figure, responsible for making rivers flow, bringing daylight to the world, hanging the moon in the sky, and acquiring fire. He also created people, and then is said to have tricked them out of their food.

Mystical powers have been attributed to Raven as far back as ancient Greece. Odin, the Raven God and ruler of the Norse gods, kept a wolf on each side of his throne and a raven on each shoulder. Wolves and ravens even accompanied Odin into battle.

The Alaskan legend of the elderberry shrub tells of the time Raven traveled along a northern river and met Stone and Elderberry, who argued over who should give birth to the Tsimshian people, the natives of Southeast Alaska. Stone argued that if she gave birth first, then the people would live an extraordinarily long time, whereas if Elderberry was first to give birth, then the people's life span would be brief. Wise Raven listened and saw that Stone was almost ready to deliver, so he reached out and touched Elderberry, instructing her to go first. She did, and that is the reason people don't live as long as stones.

🐾

The last long days of May signaled the onset of the main mosquito season. They arrived in waves of bloodsucking, buzz-bombing hordes from hell. Northern mosquitoes are larger and more aggressive than their southern relatives. Their bites raise large welts whose itching can drive a victim to the brink of insanity. A buzzing that quickly becomes a loud whine signals their arrival.

For the entire summer, the sky-filling swarms dive-bombed us to grab a blood meal at every chance. Even when we tired of the battle and escaped into our tent they waited outside, daring us to venture into their midst, and a few dozen always beat us inside. Only the female mosquitoes draw blood; they need the nourishment to lay eggs. Thus our blood was providing the means for these pests to lay more eggs, which of course meant more mosquitoes.

In response, we grabbed our industrial-strength deet repellent and smothered our exposed skin. Considering that this substance melts plastic, one has to be desperate to use it. And desperate we were. When I smeared a little deet on Charlie, though, he pulled back in indignation, even though his nose already bore numerous bites. Fortunately I was able to persuade him to accept a milder liquid; although useless to us, it kept him reasonably mosquito-free.

By the end of May, an atmosphere of trust and acceptance prevailed between the wolf pack and our camp. The wolves often sunned themselves close to Charlie's boundary or just sat in the shade watching us. Even timid Omega relaxed and frequently stood in full view instead of furtively peering at us from behind a rock. Mother, although still somewhat aloof, was less secretive and her gaze less piercing. When we washed our clothes in the stream, she was fascinated. She would stand tilting her head this way and that, as if trying to understand this strange activity. We hoped that as her trust in us increased, she would bring her pups out of the den.

Alpha, although always authoritative, proved to be a gentle leader and quickly demonstrated acceptance of Charlie after our first week at Wolf Camp One. Later his relaxed posture would exhibit acceptance of Bill and me as well. His natural gentleness, self-confidence, and assured position as his family's undisputed leader likely made it easier for him to readily accept Charlie as the alpha of his human pack. With Alpha's own role unquestioned, he felt no need to defend himself against Charlie, or even against Bill and me, and thus quickly disregarded us as a threat. In contrast, Omega, who clearly lacked self-esteem, usually kept to the edges of the pack and took as long as two months to accept Charlie and, later, Bill and me.

Easygoing Denali and Beta took little notice of us after the first two weeks. Beta, as the second in command, was never required to prove his leadership and calmly took life as it came.

As for Denali, whenever he wasn't leading a hunt or watching for prey from a ridge top, he spent his time relaxing and keeping a low, fairly unemotional profile. Always one of the last to join in a game, he played with wild abandon; he enjoyed bowling the teenagers over and then, as they jumped to their feet, whipping around to knock them down again. Even when both teens ganged up on Denali, his astonishing ability to twist and turn usually left them racing in his wake.

The mischievous, energetic teenagers soon discovered that playing was more fun than observing the neighbors. They mostly ignored Bill and me and only occasionally watched Charlie.

The seeds of trust had sprouted. It was time to plan a strategy that would enable us to observe a hunt. Already we had attempted to follow but had soon been left far behind, even when the wolves were just loping along. We would have no chance when they increased their pace as they neared prey.

At 4:30 A.M. on the last day of May, Denali, who had been scouting from the lookout since midnight, suddenly raced down the slope to greet Alpha with vigorous tail wagging. Beta and Omega quickly joined them. After a few minutes of excited milling about, the four wolves, led by Denali, trotted along the main path from the den and disappeared into the trees.

Bill, Charlie, and I had already left camp at 2 A.M., hoping that the wolves would hunt that day. We had positioned ourselves on a low rise about three hundred yards away, with an unobstructed view of the wolves' living area. We hoped our advantage of starting closer to the prey area would enable us to follow the wolves for at least part of the distance to their hunting site.

The wolves cleared the trees, trotting at a steady pace, and headed north about a mile across the tundra toward an unnamed river. Nine ravens accompanied the wolves, circling ahead and then waiting for them to catch up. We jogged along an easy shortcut across the tundra, and noticed the ravens flying ahead of the wolves as if they knew where to locate prey. Twenty minutes later, we arrived at the ice-choked river's edge.

The fifty-foot-wide river was bordered by two-foot-high earth banks. We guessed the water depth beneath the ice to be no more than six feet. A sheet of foot-thick ice covered the water, bank to bank. Although the ice was melting in the May warmth, it appeared strong enough to hold our weight. The wolves had already fanned out, crossed the ice, and disappeared into willow brush and black spruce on the far side.

Charlie, always happy at the sight of ice, bounced ahead in eager anticipation. Bill and I gingerly stepped onto the slippery surface to test its strength. After we had taken a few cautious steps, the ice settled two or three inches with a few ominous creaks and groans. We called Charlie to walk behind us for safety.

With Bill in the lead, we had reached the halfway point when suddenly a thunderous boom echoed around us. A wide chunk of ice ahead of us had collapsed a foot, and water was flooding over the top of the ice sheet. With pounding hearts we fled back in the direction we had come, Charlie racing ahead.

All around us, the ice began to sink. Urging each other to hurry, we leaped and sidestepped the gaping cracks that kept opening in our path. Suddenly my legs plunged through the ice and I found myself in freezing water to my waist. Desperate to avoid being swept under by the strong current, I threw my arms out wide across the ice, my fingers frantically clawing at its surface. The water's cold stab shocked my mind and body.

In an instant Bill thrust his trekking pole into my outstretched hand. I hung on while he pulled. I levered my body up onto the surface of the ice with my free arm. Face down, I spread my weight across the ice to prevent another plunge. After sliding the last few feet to safety with legs almost numb from the frigid water, I stumbled to the bank with Bill's help.

As I shivered uncontrollably, Bill helped me strip off my soaking clothes and boots. Under a warm sun, we vigorously rubbed circulation back into my limbs.

"Now we know why the wolves fanned out to cross the river," I said. "They were smart enough to know the ice was weaker than it looked."

Soon four ravens arrived and circled overhead as I put on the spare set of clothes I always carried in my day pack. The birds landed on a tussock mound a few feet away and cawed softly.

"Do you think they're concerned by our close call?" I whispered.

"If they are, I'm ready to believe anything," Bill said.

Two ravens waddled toward us through the cotton grass, still chatting quietly. Charlie lay down, making no attempt to approach them. Considering his intense dislike of the birds, we were surprised.

As I finished dressing, two ravens hopped to within six feet of us, still cawing gently. Soon all four circled us on the ground, talking softly, their black eyes fixed on us. After ten minutes of circling, the ravens flew to the top branches of a spruce tree and raised their voices in a loud, hard-edged cackle.

A wolf—Alpha—howled from the far bank. Surprised, we turned to see four wolves looking on as Alpha howled again. A few flaps of the ravens' huge wings lofted them over the river to the trees above the wolves. As the wolves disappeared into the forest, the ravens followed overhead. A quarter of a mile away the ravens circled once, then descended below treetop level to what we presumed was a kill site.

Mystified, we pulled out our snacks and tried to make sense of all that had transpired. "The ravens and wolves must have been close enough to hear us shouting," Bill said, munching on a handful of peanuts. "They must have sensed that we were in trouble."

"The ravens seemed concerned," I agreed. "But what about the wolves? How do they fit in?"

The ravens understood our predicament, we guessed, and as soon as the crisis was over had called the wolves. The two howls seemed to represent some sort of communication between the species.

"Remember Billy McCaw and what he told us about ravens?" I said as we headed back to camp.

Billy was an elder of the Gwich'in First Nation whom we had met two years ago. He had told us that wolves and ravens talked to each other. So old he could not remember his own age, Billy had spoken to us in a raspy voice with a faraway look in his faded eyes. "Ravens call the wolves and lead them to prey," he said. "After the wolves eat, the birds take what's left. Ravens will call the wolves to an injured animal too. They know more than all the animals in the north."

When I asked him if ravens helped humans to hunt, he had replied, "Sometimes they do. It is said that they will help only those who respect them. It is said that a long time ago my grandfather's dogsled overturned and hurt his leg. Ravens who followed him on the hunt flew two miles back, and screeched and circled until his brother paid attention and followed them to my grandfather. Many of our elders can tell when a raven is serious and is talking."

Now we understood what Billy meant. After witnessing what appeared to be their real concern over our welfare, we could no longer regard the ravens merely as a camp nuisance. We would always remember them as our friends and protectors.

Above

At 5 A.M. IN THE FIRST WEEK OF JUNE, four of the wolves gathered at the den to set out on a hunt. After the usual lively display of tail wagging and what looked like smiling—the corners of their mouths were turned up slightly—Denali began a brief howling session. The others soon joined in, joyful and exuberant. They frisked around Mother, rubbing her shoulders and licking her muzzle. After several minutes they headed out: Beta and Alpha, with Denali in the lead and Mother following right behind him.

Hoping they had located prey close by, we hastily grabbed our day packs and set out. But ten minutes from the den, just as we reached a right-hand turn in the trail, we met Mother striding confidently in front, bringing the group back home. They veered off the trail to avoid us while Charlie, who was leading Bill and me, made a quick left into the trees. Having averted a head-on meeting, we allowed the wolves to pass, then puzzled at the sudden turn of events.

Back at the den, the three males affectionately licked Mother's muzzle. After a few minutes she disappeared inside, and the others departed once more.

"Mother must have had a sudden change of heart," Bill said.

I was thinking of the pups. "I bet she had second thoughts about leaving the kids at home while she went off hunting."

"Well, if we're going to keep up, we'd better hustle," Bill said. "They're already into the trees."

We need not have worried. Only two hundred yards away, we came upon all three wolves digging a large hole to one side of the trail at an astonishing rate. Wolves' reputation as diggers has no equal. With heads down and paws flying, all three soon had dug a hole the size of a bathtub into the soft earth. Then for no apparent reason they all stopped, sniffed the edges, and raised their legs to aim jets of urine into the center. Having engaged in this mysterious group activity, they headed off once more with Denali in the lead.

After inspecting the hole to nowhere and finding no purpose for it, we continued onward. Charlie added his own signatures, one on each side of the hole.

Even when hunting, the wolves displayed their natural, unconstrained curiosity. As we hurried along after the pack, we saw a wolf now and then stop briefly, paw at something only he could see, and then run to catch up. Occasionally all three stopped to inspect small rocks in the woods. Or one would pause to scent-mark a bent old tree or a lichen-covered rock that no doubt had seen many years of scent-marking. Denali picked up a spruce stick and carried this prize for some distance, dropping it only when he reached the open tundra. Fresh bear scat on the trail caught their attention too, but proved to be of only momentary interest.

The wolves traveled without urgency, as though they knew their prey would be there for the chase. They stopped frequently to raise sensitive noses to test the breeze for scent.

We gradually fell behind. Charlie tugged hard at his leash, impatient with our slow pace. After he almost pulled me off my feet Bill helped restrain him, but our combined efforts barely contained his impressive strength. We jogged behind the wolves as they veered off to the north through a shadowed valley bordered by steep rock. Ahead the wolves were already out in the open on rolling tundra. We continued to jog on as the trail faded into the pathless wilderness, but the threesome was now too distant to follow.

We realized that if we were ever going to reach a hunt site, we would have to change tactics. As we snacked on dried fruit before heading back to camp to await the wolves, we discussed our options. First of all, we had to figure out where the wolves usually hunted and which route they traveled to get there. "Our only hope is to wait at a place where the wolves usually pass, then take a shortcut to where they're headed," I said, hoping I sounded more optimistic than I felt. The wolves' ability to out-distance us so easily was discouraging.

"That's no easy task," said Bill, ever practical. "But if we find a high place along their most-used route, it might work."

For the next several days, we followed the wolves every time a group left the den. We soon discovered a frequently used junction three-quarters of a mile away: a two-foot-high rock and an ancient tree snag at the edge of the tundra. Both were heavily scent-marked and surrounded by numerous wolf scats left by passing hunters. From this point the wolves would branch off in several directions, some-times following faint trails

Charlie sits in our tent doorway as he watches the wolves play.

but most often heading across the trail-less tundra. The junction sat beneath an easily climbed three-hundred-foot ridge. We decided to start waiting on top every morning for the wolves to pass by on their way to hunt.

The next few mornings we sacrificed sleep to rise at 1 A.M. and hike to our lookout, but we soon grew frustrated when the wolves chose other routes. Finally, one calm morning in mid-June, as we sat on the ridge munching a food bar for breakfast, our patience was rewarded.

Denali, Alpha, Omega, and Beta stopped at the junction. Together they scent-marked both the tree snag and the rock. Then, after Alpha and Denali vigorously scratched up patches of dirt, the four fanned out to stalk three moose that browsed a half mile away on the open tundra. We scrambled down the ridge and set out. But no sooner had we cleared the trees than all four wolves stopped, heads raised, listening. We strained to catch the sound, but heard only silence. Suddenly the panicked wolves raced past us, melting into the deep shadows of the trees and cliffs.

Sensing danger, we ran back into the trees, not understanding what we were running from. The wolves had fled something only they could hear. Moments later the faint hum of an aircraft approaching from the north drifted toward us. We pressed our bodies, with Charlie behind us, against a rock wall shielded by trees. A few feet away the wolves crouched to the ground, concealed in the dark shadows.

A green-and-white airplane equipped with large tundra tires approached directly overhead. With a loud drone that echoed off the mountains, the plane climbed to avoid the steep ridge protecting us and the wolves. Two men gazed down, rifles protruding through the open side windows: They were hunting wolves from the air.

The plane circled again. Although confident its occupants wouldn't shoot at us, we stayed motionless to avoid attracting attention to the wolves. They lay still as stone, their coats blending with the surroundings. After another low pass, the plane veered to the east and vanished. The four wolves cautiously rose, stepped into the sunlight, and tilted their heads to listen. Satisfied that the danger had passed, they made a beeline back to the den, in single file, with Alpha in the lead.

We quickly returned to our camp and found the entire family hidden inside the den and dugouts. Two hours later, Alpha and Denali emerged from their hiding places but remained nervous for the rest of the day. None of the wolves played games, lay in the sun, or climbed the ridges. Instead they stayed close to cover. A subdued Alpha climbed to a rocky ledge and sat alone for several hours, as if ready to protect his family. Mother remained in the den with her pups and didn't appear until the next morning.

Although our camp was concealed by ridges, we moved our blue-green tent under a large overhanging rock buttress to make sure no aerial hunters would see us. We also placed willow branches over the tent and latrine cover.

"I bet the rest of the family we saw last year was shot by aerial hunters," Bill said sadly.

It seemed likely. At Eagle Plains we had noticed an airplane equipped with tires large enough to allow landings on the soft tundra. Two hunters equipped with guns had boarded the airplane. Bill asked the pilot what they were hunting. "Wolves," the pilot replied. Did they shoot wolves from the air? The pilot had nodded defiantly as he ground his cigarette butt into the earth. "As many of the darned pests as we can find."

"I hate having to stand by, not being able to do anything to stop it," Bill said, his rage boiling to the surface. "Perhaps they were attacked more than once." He shook his head in frustration.

I, too, felt angry and frustrated about what our wolf friends had already gone through, and what they might have to experience again. It seemed so unfair. What pleasure could anyone get from callously slaughtering innocent animals?

I watched Alpha stand guard. "At least the survivors have learned their lesson well, and they know to run at the first sound of a plane."

We could only imagine the aerial chase it must have taken to kill half the family. Since the mountains and high ridges made it impossible to fly low over the den, we suspected that the wolves were attacked on the open tundra while on a hunt, and some hadn't been able to reach safety in time.

Charlie seemed to have picked up on our despondency. Depressed and unresponsive, he lay on my sleeping bag with his head on his paws. Did he sense the danger his wolf friends had faced? That night he showed no interest in dinner, and ate only when I sat with him and fed him from my hand. Not until the next afternoon did he return to his normal self.

Aerial hunting for wolves has been a controversial subject in the Yukon Territory and Alaska, as well as in the rest of the United States, for many years. Wolves caught on open ground have little chance against a small aircraft that can easily outmaneuver them. As a result, entire packs are often wiped out. In helicopters or in planes with wide tundra tires, hunters can land, gather the pelts, and return home to show off their "trophies."

This hunting method has caused such public outrage that it has been frequently banned, but under pressure from hunters, officials have worked to undermine and eventually rescind such bans. Even when outlawed, aerial hunting has continued; in wide-open, sparsely populated areas such as the Yukon, lawbreakers are difficult to locate.

Historically, gray wolves ranged over the prairies, forests, and tundra of North America, Europe, and Asia. But as their prey species were eliminated by human hunters, and as human populations grew worldwide, the wolves' range became more confined and they were forced to exploit domestic sheep and cattle. This in turn made the wolves more despised by humans.

The last wolf in Europe was killed around 1950, but wolves everywhere have suffered persecution and elimination. Extermination practices have ranged from shooting to trapping

Denali leads a hunt.

and poisoning. Many other species, such as bear, lynx, and eagles, have also fallen to such poisoning. In some of America's lower forty-eight states wolves have been forced into extinction, while in other states the animals have survived only because they have been concealed by wilderness.

In 1907 an official order was issued to the U.S. Army authorizing the killing of all predator species in Yellowstone National Park's 2.2 million acres, including wolves, mountain lions, and coyotes. The army and the National Park Service proceeded to exterminate wolves in a relentless campaign that used barbaric methods such as strychnine poisoning and burning. They even used crying pups as bait to attract adult wolves, who were then shot as they attempted to rescue the pups. Elsewhere, Glacier National Park's native wolf population was exterminated by the late 1920s. In Alaska wolves are still being killed by aerial hunters.

The wolves of Canada's Yukon Territories have suffered a similar fate. In Canada, wolves are often killed in government-sanctioned programs, the reasoning being that reducing the wolf population will allow moose and caribou populations to increase, which will benefit hunters. But because of the vast areas of wilderness in many Canadian provinces, the wolf continues to survive. The wolf population nationwide may be in excess of 50,000, and in spite of many people's desire to exterminate all the wolves in the Yukon, government statistics estimate that 4,500 remained as of the year 2000.

Many remote areas, such as Siberia and the mountains of many Asian countries, contain thousands of wolves, thanks to the regions' inaccessibility to aerial hunters. In Mongolia, wolves exist in healthy numbers of around 11,000. Herdsmen there still use guard dogs to protect their livestock from wolf predators.

Pockets of wolves survive in low numbers in other countries. Several hundred live in Greece and Turkey, and perhaps as many as a thousand live in the mountains of Iran and India. It is thought that a sturdy population exists in northern China, but no survey has ever been conducted.

In our travels among native cultures, people have told us of their ancestors' reverence of the wolf as one of the most sacred animals. Wolves are honored in native legends and folklore for their bravery, their will to survive, and their hunting prowess. Some native cultures acknowledge a high degree of parallelism between wolves and humans.

When Bill and I trekked 1,450 miles across the Mongolian Gobi Desert in 2001, we discovered that while the nomads spoke of wolves with reverence, they also hunted them as a status symbol to prove personal bravery. Mongolians proudly told us that they were the sons of the blue wolf, who descended from heaven and took as his wife a fallow doe. They believed their great leader Genghis Khan was also descended from the blue wolf. "If you see a wolf in January, you will have good luck for a whole year," an elderly nomad told us. Another Mongolian told us the wolf tail is sacred, and drinking the warm blood of a wolf promotes good health.

Back at our camp, we talked about the day's events. "Now we know why the wolves look skyward," I said. We had thought they were keeping an eye open for ravens and their dive-bombing assaults, but noticed that they often looked up even when birds were nowhere in sight. In fact, the pack had developed this habit to protect themselves from aerial hunters and had taught it to their offspring. It was evidence that wolves gather information from unnatural, life-threatening events and pass that knowledge on to ensure their pack's survival, indicating that they have an intelligence capable of adapting to survive.

After three days the family's behavior gradually returned to normal. On the fifth day they resumed their usual hunting routine. But from then on our ears, like those of the wolves, were always alert for the terrible sound of an approaching airplane.

Hunt

ONE MID-JUNE EVENING as they surveyed the distant tundra from their vantage point high on the den ridge, Omega and Denali spied six white Dall sheep a half mile away. Quickly joined by Beta and Alpha, they left for the hunt, led by Denali.

From where we waited above the junction, we watched the wolves with binoculars. They trotted toward us in single file on the well-worn trail through thin patches of spruce trees. In a grassy clearing, Beta stopped midstride, his body low to the ground, and crept toward a quarry that moved in the foot-high tundra grass. Suddenly he pounced to snatch a squealing lemming. In moments its struggles ceased. After tossing the tiny gray body into the air in an attempt at play, Beta caught it, crunched, and swallowed. Although we felt sorry for the lemming, we reminded ourselves that wolves observe nature's way. The wolves were always on the lookout for small snacks they might find on their way to a hunt.

The four wolves were in no hurry. The sheep, upwind, remained unaware and continued to graze placidly on grasses and sedges a few hundred yards away. The hunters continued along the trail, occasionally scent-marking a tree or a rock. Once Denali abruptly leaped a few feet to one side to examine some imagined movement, then he hurried back to lead his companions forward along the trail. Finally they arrived at the junction below our lookout spot on the ridge, and thoroughly scent-marked the old snag and the rock.

Meanwhile, two sheep lay down to rest. All four wolves crouched, heads up, ears forward, watching their prey. In a few minutes, Denali and the others fanned out, with bodies slung low, beginning their patient, deliberate approach.

Suddenly aware of the danger only a hundred feet away, the six sheep leaped to attention, legs braced, facing the wolves. One stamped its foot in defiance. Then, as one, they bolted for a ridge to the east. The four wolves raced after the sheep. The hunters and the hunted dashed across the rocks, surefooted and magnificent. As the sheep crested the first low ridge, one stopped to face the pursuers, but in a moment he fled with the others, who suddenly swerved toward us.

The wolves split up. Denali and Omega swung through a shortcut to head off the sheep. The other two ran behind to herd them forward. The sheep dashed along a faint trail, desperate to escape, their white bodies propelled on agile limbs that took no notice of the steep slope.

Just as all six reached the crest, Denali and Omega burst across the ridge, heads thrust forward, legs pumping, only a few yards behind the sheep. Then Denali abruptly stopped. Omega, still at full speed, crashed into his shoulder. Alpha and Beta raced up the slope, stopping when they encountered Denali and Omega standing motionless.

The sheep swept past a hundred feet from us and bounded in long leaps down the back side of the ridge, then up the next. They paused a moment to look back at the wolves, who now trotted with apparent indifference to the hunt. The sheep moved away, no longer fleeing the wolves, who had turned from predators into mere observers. It was as if a signal had passed between the two species that the hunt was off.

The sheep and wolves disappeared over another ridge. A half hour later the four ambled back, stopping now and then to scent-mark. They lay down a hundred feet away on the ridge where we waited, looking in the direction the sheep had disappeared but showing no desire to resume the chase.

As the unexpected turn of events swirled about us, we could only stare, incredulous, and anticipate the wolves' next move. After some time, when it was clear that the wolves had changed their minds—at least as far as these six sheep were concerned—and no further action would be forthcoming, we took out snacks.

Twelve opportunistic ravens who had flown from tree to tree ahead of the wolves, expecting to share in the hunt leftovers, now perched on the surrounding rocks, voicing their disappointment in cacophonous tones. A furious Charlie chased one impudent bird after it brazenly brushed his head. He lunged at the raven, but with a rasping cry it triumphantly hopped onto a ledge, barely out of reach, and cawed. Charlie shot it a murderous look, then walked to our side and sat down with his back to the bird.

All twenty-four raven eyes were now fixed on our food. Their rasping caws rose to a deafening level. Hoping to quiet them, we tossed a few crackers on the ground. The volume lowered. One individual, chatting nonstop short caws as if in deep conversation with me, hopped to within a foot of my outstretched hand. I traded two crackers for bird gossip.

Charlie, an exhilarated spectator of the hunt, had kept up a barrage of barks while the chase continued, but he calmed as soon as it ended. Although Bill and I were confused by what we had seen, Charlie seemed unperturbed, appearing to understand all. When the wolves returned, he took no further interest in the sheep.

Surprised that what had appeared to be an eminently successful hunt had been abruptly called off, we concluded that there must have been some sort of communication between the sheep and the wolves. Wolves often test their prey and usually attack only if they see a weakness. Given the ready supply of prey here, these wolves apparently weren't willing to waste their energy on animals that showed so much speed and strength. For their part, the sheep wouldn't have stopped to look back unless they were sure the wolves had given up the chase.

The four wolves napped in the shade of the rocks until Alpha rose, stretched his sleek body, then set off alone across the rocky terrain, scent-marking at frequent intervals as he went. Every few days, and always after a rainstorm, Alpha—sometimes alone, but often accompanied by the teenagers—renewed his scent marks.

As Alpha disappeared, the rest of the wolves sauntered down the slope they had raced up only an hour before, stopping occasionally to scan the tundra for more hunting prospects. There were none, so they made their way back home at a leisurely pace, stopping once in a while to scent-mark a

Catching an early morning scent of prey.

tree or rock. The three wolves also stopped when Beta found a stick and taunted the other two into chasing him for the prize. After a merry chase and an energetic tug-of-war in which the stick was reduced to slivers, they continued, zigzagging now and then to examine something of interest. Omega found another stick and carried it to the den, presumably to use as a future toy. The ravens also returned, perching in the trees and on the ridges to await further hunting opportunities.

The rest of the day passed quietly. I devoted thirteen journal pages to the morning's events, while Bill repaired the stove that had sputtered to a halt as we brewed our lunchtime cup of tea. He finally found the culprit: a gasket in the fuel pump.

About 8 P.M., Beta and the teenagers headed off toward a notch in the ridge behind our camp. Because our supply of Labrador tea had run out, we decided to follow the trio and perhaps collect tea leaves from a new area.

The aromatic, leathery leaves of the Labrador tea plant, a common northern shrub, were used by native peoples to ease the symptoms of colds, indigestion, and food poisoning. Trappers and fur traders used Labrador leaves as a substitute for British black tea. On a previous northern journey, an elderly Gwich'in woman had instructed us to brew the leaves very lightly. Excessive brewing releases ledol, she explained, a toxin that causes dizziness and even death if the tea is brewed for long periods and drunk to excess.

We took a shortcut and dropped down the backside of the ridge, only a few yards behind the wolves. They continued toward a trickling stream that flowed through spruce and willow thickets. Beyond, we discovered a beaver-made glassy pond at least ten feet deep set amid a mossy marsh. Calling upon their impressive construction skills, the resourceful animals had felled small spruce and used the trees and countless willow branches to make a thirty-foot, S-shaped dam. They built their lodge inside the dam, which they entered through underwater tunnels to discourage any predators from following. All the streams in the area had been dammed by beavers at some point along their length to form numerous ponds of various sizes, where the beavers then built lodges and raised their young.

A dark gray beaver, his wet coat gleaming, worked energetically to saw a fallen log with his impressive self-sharpening teeth. He stopped to watch the approaching wolves. Then, sensing danger, he instantly escaped with a splash to the safety of the lake. The delighted wolves, with Yukon in the lead, raced to the water's edge in a futile attempt to catch the beaver, who swam to the center of the pond and watched the antics of the wolves as they splashed and leaped through the shallow water at the shore.

A few minutes later, delight turned to frustration as the pack realized its quarry had escaped. They returned to the bank, shook themselves dry, and paced as three more adult beavers and two kits quietly slid into the water. The adults immediately formed a protective circle around the kits while keeping their black eyes fixed on the unwelcome intruders.

Apparently beavers were not high on Charlie's list of animals to chase. He showed no interest in the furry rodents and instead concentrated on excavating the burrow of some tiny creature. Disappointed to find no one at home there, he tugged at his leash to signal that it was time to move on. We suspected that Charlie's dislike of water was the main reason for his disinterest in the beavers.

Beavers, the largest of North American rodents, can grow to around seventy pounds. Family oriented, they commit to life-long pairing during their ten-year life span. Their lodges, made of sticks, small branches, and mud, have underwater entrances to protect against predators, while their living quarters are high and dry. These herbivorous, nonhibernating animals cache fresh branches to serve as a winter food supply. They also eat aquatic plants, roots, and bark, and use tree trunks for building material. Although their underwater tunnels are their safe havens, they are hunted by wolves, bears, and sometimes lynx.

Further investigation of the area surrounding the pond revealed deep canals dug into the soft earth, where the industrious beavers had floated four-inch-diameter logs to the pond. The beavers' influence on the landscape, as they dammed streams to create ponds and wetlands, was clearly beneficial to many aquatic species.

After half an hour the frustrated wolves finally gave up on the beavers and returned to the den. We suspected that the beavers were used to their visits.

Bill, Charlie, and I continued across the beaver wetlands to the edge of a muskeg area, where we found the ground-hugging Labrador tea growing in profusion. We picked a week's supply of the leaves and set off again into what we thought was fairly dry muskeg, but quickly ran into trouble. Leading the way, Bill had traveled only ten feet when he suddenly sank halfway to his knees in the sticky brown peat.

I shoved my trekking pole toward his outstretched hand as I grabbed a nearby stunted black spruce to use as a brace. Bill struggled mightily to stay on the surface of the muck. After ten more minutes of fighting for toeholds, he reached the relatively solid patch of earth where Charlie and I stood. We quickly retreated to the safety of more stable ground.

Muskeg wetlands, sometimes hundreds of years old, contain plants in various stages of decay and usually form in wet, poorly drained areas. Decomposition of dead plants is slow due to the water-saturated, acidic soils. Therefore, the accumulation of decomposing debris builds up to form peat. Wetland is reclassified as muskeg when one foot of peat has accumulated, and it can take a thousand years to build. In some areas of the Yukon and Alaska, peat is twenty feet thick.

Muskeg itself, a floating mat that covers a bog, can be dangerous, as we had just discovered. The underlying soggy peat is frequently deep and lacks toeholds. Victims who are unable to climb out may meet a suffocating end. The only safe time to traverse muskeg is during the frozen winter.

"From now on we'll forage around the edges with the bears, wolves, and lemmings," Bill said, sounding as though he'd had enough. "No more shortcuts across muskeg." As the shortcut had been my suggestion, I thought it prudent to remain silent.

After we scraped most of the brown slime off Bill's pants, we returned to camp by a new route across the tundra. We climbed a low rise on which a lone wind-blasted spruce, twisted and bent, desperately clung to life. A narrow lake sparkled, almost hidden between two ridges. A startled loon skittered to lift from the water, and the maniacal cry of another pierced the stillness. Then the immeasurable calm returned. We continued our concealed watch as a half-dozen loons floated peacefully on the water, their voices breaking into wails, gentle coos, and eerie laughs.

A Siberian Eskimo legend tells us that when the world was covered in water, Loon dove to the bottom and surfaced with enough mud to make Earth. These birds are the strongest and deepest swimmers of all, and can dive more than five hundred feet. To reach such depths, they squeeze the air out from under their feathers and deflate their lungs. As we watched from our vantage point, a mother with a chick riding safely on her back slid into the water and paddled away as ripples gently radiated across the lake.

An hour later, we arrived at our camp. After a dinner of rice, beans, dried fruit, and Labrador tea, I spent the next hour writing journal notes. Bill washed the muskeg peat from his pants and sewed a button onto his shirt. Then, taking Charlie with him, he climbed the slope behind our tent. They soon returned with the verdict that a ridge to the west that we hadn't yet crossed looked interesting. We decided to explore early the next morning.

I was eager to look for not only cotton grass roots, which Bill and I had sampled before and found delicious, but also lichens. Since caribou eat lichen, I reasoned, it should be good for us too. At the mention of lichen, Bill merely rolled his eyes skyward at the thought of another gastronomical experiment in the name of nutrition. During our many years of marriage, he had patiently suffered through countless such efforts.

At 5 A.M. we marched toward a threatening sky, shaking the cobwebs of sleep from our minds. A gray fog washed across the mountaintops, swirling about the narrow caribou trails that laced the slopes.

Dall sheep are always of interest to Charlie.

As we reached an area of head-high dense willows, move-ment flashed in the undergrowth. Charlie instantly leaped, snarling and lunging and almost tearing his leash from my hands. We peered ahead, expecting a bear, but instead saw a gray catlike figure crouched over a freshly killed hare under a canopy of tangled willows. Bill grabbed Charlie's leash as well, and we both hung on while Bill maneuvered the end of the leash around a tree that would act as a belay to stop Charlie's wild charge.

With Charlie secure, I quickly grabbed my camera to photo-graph the lynx, whose growls were becoming louder and more vicious. He was determined not to abandon his dinner. The fury in his luminous green eyes spelled attack. I barely managed a few fast frames before we retreated, hauling a snarling Charlie behind us.

Lynx are as quiet as a falling snowflake, hidden and secre-tive. They are striking creatures, clothed in mottled, thick gray fur, adorned with long black ear tufts, their short tails tipped with black. Usually we saw little more than a silent blur as they melted into the shadows. Strictly carnivorous, their main prey is the snowshoe hare. Lynx numbers are directly connected to the abundance of hare populations. These wild cats silently stalk on thick-furred paws that allow them to speed over barren ground or snow.

As we skirted the lynx, a disappointed Charlie lunged again at the crouched, snarling cat. Only when we neared the ridge did he turn his attention to a group of Dall ewes and lambs. When the sheep caught sight of us, they disappeared into the swirling fog. The ledges, although only inches wide, were sufficient for their nimble feet.

At four hundred feet, we hastened through a heavy mist that merged with dark clouds, then dropped into a lonely meadow full of cotton grass, its snowy heads waving in the increasing breeze. Keeping one eye on the sky, we dug as many roots as our plastic bag would hold, then headed to camp the way we had come.

Cotton grass is an important forage food of northern native peoples all across Alaska and the Yukon. Two years ago we had met a Gwich'in woman collecting cotton grass roots not far from Dawson City. To satisfy our curiosity, she allowed us to eat the sweet root. Ever since then, we have looked forward to the treat whenever we travel to Alaska or northern Canada. The peeled root can be eaten raw and makes a gourmet addition to a bowl of rice.

Along the way, I picked a large handful of gray-green lichen and stuffed the fibrous vegetation into my pack. "There's no way we can eat that stuff," Bill felt the need to comment. I made no reply as I pondered how I might soften the leatherlike growth.

We reached Wolf Camp One just as a sudden clap of thunder rent the heavens, sending three ravens squawking skyward in confused flight. As the startled birds dove back to the protection of the trees, we sprinted for our tent, dodging huge raindrops. The wolves had already taken shelter in the dugouts and Mother was in the den with the pups.

As the storm beat down on our tent and the thunder rolled above us, Charlie lolled across my sleeping bag. Bill wrote journal notes while I lit the stove, brewed Labrador tea, and peeled cotton grass roots. A liberal helping of peanut butter smeared on salted crackers completed our modest meal.

I took the lichen and pulled it apart to taste it, then handed some to Bill. "Pretty tasteless but chewy," he said. "Glad we're not caribou and don't have to live on it." Lichen, a slow-growing plant, does not require soil. It gleans its nutrients from the air and tolerates the extremely low Arctic temperatures. Although not a moss, it is sometimes referred to as reindeer moss and, along with other lichens, is a vital food for musk ox and moose as well as caribou.

At dinnertime, while Bill took inventory of our food and fuel supplies and Charlie napped, I cooked rice and furtively added finely chopped lichen, along with freeze-dried peas I hoped would disguise my secret. "Boy, this tastes good," Bill said. "It's got a sort of slight musky taste."

I laughed.

"Lichen! You sneaked it in!" he said, laughing at my audacity. "I should have known you wouldn't give up."

After years of expeditions together, Bill and I knew each other well. Our different personalities allowed us to think and act separately but also work as a team when necessary. We quickly learned that fussing over small things was a waste of time and energy. Bill's quiet nature and my chattiness blended well. My habit of getting things done yesterday was tempered over the years by Bill's more realistic attitude that sometimes tomorrow will do just fine.

We had met in New Zealand in 1959, three weeks after Bill's company sent him there from his home country, the

United States, to fly a helicopter in New Zealand's agriculture industry. I was impressed by his straightforward, honest approach to life. We immediately became good friends and discovered many similar interests. Our relationship culminated in a church wedding in July 1961, complete with a long white bridal gown I designed and made myself. (At that time I had my own business designing bridal and formal wear.)

That August we left New Zealand, when Bill was assigned to fly for the next four years in Guatemala and Honduras. While there, we lived in jungle compounds guarded twenty-four hours a day to keep marauding antigovernment rebels at bay, an experience that prepared us somewhat for our later expeditions to remote, little traveled, sometimes dangerous places in the world. In Central America we quickly became a balanced team, which has served us well over the years.

That night the rain sputtering against our tent reminded us of storms at home in the rugged and dramatic North Cascades. Thunder echoed from far away, and clouds swept across the mountains. The nearby stream rose a foot as it gurgled and swirled. As we drifted off to sleep to the comforting sounds of the rain, we looked forward to spending time with Margaret in a few weeks, when we would be meeting her to replenish our dwindling provisions. Only a quarter of the way through the summer portion of our expedition, we already had so many stories to tell.

Invasion

WITH THE ARRIVAL OF THE SUMMER SOLSTICE on June 21, the sun turned up its heat to 80 degrees Fahrenheit. Hunting hours shifted to early morning, late evening, or night. The wolves visited the stream more frequently. They lay on their stomachs on the gravel bars, front legs stretched out before them, lapping water as they cooled their bodies. They emerged with huge shakes of their coats, rolling in the moss and coarse grass. Although Charlie detested water, he splashed in his own nearby sector of the stream, sometimes at the same time as the wolves, as if to share the activity.

As we watched Charlie enter the stream, we could see that he wanted to copy the wolves to gain acceptance, although he had a definite fear of water. I had first discovered this when we walked together to the magnetic North Pole. He displayed excessive caution when crossing any area of broken ice where water was visible. His intelligence told him that to fall in could mean death. Whenever we crossed a rushing stream a few feet deep in the Cascade Range, we always had to look for a crossing with a fallen log that Charlie could walk across.

Sometimes hunting wolves returned with their muzzles and parts of their fur covered in the prey's blood. This was often an occasion for a bath, wolf style. They flopped down in the shallow water of the stream and let the stains flow from their coats, paws, and muzzles. Then came the customary shaking and rolling in the grass to dry their fur.

A wolf's splendid coat has two layers. Dense underfur lies next to the skin, while another top layer of coarse, long, dark-tipped guard hairs sheds water and keeps the underfur dry. With the arrival of spring temperatures, much of the undercoat is shed. The most luxurious portion lies across the shoulders, where the guard hairs are the longest. A wolf's legs are covered with short, thinner hair. Charlie's coat closely resembled a wolf's; in the winter it grew so dense we could hardly work our fingers down to his skin. Long black guard hairs covered his back and shoulders.

One breezy, mosquito-free afternoon, after the wolves had consumed the sheep of the previous night's hunt, the usual air of contentment settled over the pack. They lay about sleeping among the rocks and trees, or just lounging in hollows they had dug in the soft dirt. One might change position now and then, or rise to dig a little more to increase the comfort of the bed. Charlie was fast asleep in his mossy spot, his only sign of life an occasional twitch of a leg.

The prevailing languor was contagious. We spread out our mats for a relaxed afternoon. But soon Bill nudged me awake to watch Klondike cautiously sneaking up on Denali, who was dead to the world. When only three feet from him, Klondike turned her back and dug dirt that hurtled through the air to whack Denali in the head. Denali instantly leaped to his feet with an indignant yelp. He struggled to focus his sleepy eyes on his tormentor, who, now that she had achieved the desired reaction, raced up the ridge. He sprinted and caught her. They were instantly entangled in a wrestling embrace. With growls and yelps, they rolled together all the way to the bottom of the ridge, landing close to the den entrance. Once there, they calmly stood, shook themselves clean, and strolled back to their respective beds to resume their lazy afternoon. It had all been just another game.

In the meantime a few heads rose to check out the ruckus, but none of the wolves had the energy or interest to join in. Peace continued to reign until early evening, when the pack woke up. Denali and Beta, after a short howling duet, climbed the ridge to watch for prey. The rest played games, chewed a few bones, and waited for the next hunt.

One afternoon Yukon and Klondike investigated a weather-beaten log in the creek. They played chase around it until Yukon climbed on top. Klondike saw her chance. She pushed with her nose while Yukon frantically tried to keep her balance. Just when Yukon was about to fall off, play suddenly stopped. Klondike spied a small fish. She leaped up beside Yukon and dipped her paw into the water, but the fish was in no danger, even when the two wolves jumped into the stream and chased it.

Klondike quickly gave up the chase and flopped down to amuse herself by snapping at the ripples that flowed past. Not to be outdone, Yukon jumped from the bank onto Klondike's back and, with a victorious growl, grabbed her fur ruff. The game quickly turned serious, erupting into a full-scale fight. Denali charged into the water, grabbed Klondike by the scruff of her neck, and flipped her onto the bank. Then he grabbed Yukon's ruff, dragged her out of the water, and stood over the two, snarling with bared teeth.

The teenagers collapsed onto their backs, exposing their bellies and whimpering. In a few minutes Denali left them. With tails tucked under their bodies, the two thoroughly subdued teens slunk away to a dugout to lick themselves dry. An hour later, all was forgotten and play resumed.

We observed a similar drama many times. Squabbles between the youngsters weren't tolerated by the adults, who always jumped into the fray and disciplined the offenders. But animosity never prevailed for long; quarrels were quickly forgotten.

Occasionally members of the wolf family lay close to the scent-marked boundary to watch us. Their abundant curiosity and observance of detail was a marvel. When Bill and I were the subject of their attention, it was impossible to ignore their piercing stares, which seemed to strip away all human pretense and lay bare our souls. Sometimes they observed us with heads resting on front paws, while at other times they sat alert, with heads raised, so as not to miss a single move.

Mostly, though, they ignored Bill and me, instead studying Charlie, but with a different expression—not the curious stare Bill and I rated, but a soft look that spoke of friendship, even fondness. At times a wolf communicated with Charlie by low yips and whines. Charlie responded with similar sounds, his tail fanning gently back and forth. He often sat closer to the boundary to eye his neighbors thoughtfully. A peaceful understanding had developed between them.

Out of respect for the scent-marked boundary, we avoided stepping over it. Whenever we left camp, we crossed the boundary opposite the den. The wolves appeared to respect Charlie's sector, at least when we were close by. We put our belongings inside with the door zipped shut when we were gone, just in case. But the wolves' restless curiosity and the temptation to explore our campsite ultimately proved too difficult for them to resist.

One day, to verify our suspicion that the wolves were inspecting our area in our absence, we trekked away from the den by our usual route. Once out of sight in the trees, we hurried through a low notch that led us to the back of the ridge, then climbed to the crest in a breeze that allowed us to remain downwind. After a thirty-minute wait, Alpha and Beta hesitantly walked halfway to the tent, stopped to reassure themselves that we were out of sight, then slowly approached and sniffed all around the doorway. Mother, with Denali, Omega, and the two teenagers following single file, joined Alpha and Beta, stopping now and then to look back to where we had disappeared. Their cautious posture clearly showed that they knew they were trespassing in Charlie's territory.

Just as the group became fully engrossed in a sniffing inspection of the tent, we rushed down the ridge, yelling at the top of our lungs and loudly beating a saucepan with a metal spoon that we had carried just in case our suspicions proved correct. Charlie, in the lead, voiced his indignation with angry barks and teeth-baring snaps and snarls directed at the invaders. Led by Alpha, the pack fled.

As he growled and barked his disgust, Charlie renewed his scent. The wolves seemed embarassed. Even when he faced the wolves and directly barked at them, they refused to face him and looked away, pretending to be occupied with some distant object while Mother disappeared into the refuge of the den, where she still kept the pups out of sight.

If they chose, the wolves could have shredded the tent and all our belongings in minutes. But our staged departure, intended to show them that they were not safe just because they couldn't see us, seemed to have the desired effect. Alpha lost his proud pose under Charlie's indignant protests and climbed the den ridge. With his back to us, he appeared to scan the horizon for prey, but his embarrassment was evident as he peeked over his shoulder now and then at Charlie. It was an hour before he returned to rejoin his family as if nothing had occurred. From then on, although we always left some small object outside the tent as a test whenever we left camp, the wolves seldom disturbed it.

In spite of their enduring curiosity, the wolves' high level of intelligence and strict code of social behavior reduced their temptation to invade Charlie's territory or to attack our tent when we were out of sight. The hierarchical structure of a pack lends the group cohesion as well as discipline. One of the many ways a wild wolf pack differs from a captive one is that in order to survive, a wild pack must respect their neighbors' hunting territory. Charlie's claimed area was apparently regarded the same way as a neighboring pack's home ground would be.

At the end of June, after nine weeks at the den, we erected the antenna and radioed Margaret at 6 P.M., the time she always listened in case we called. "We're ready for our resupply," I told her through the static.

"I'll meet you in three days," she replied.

On resupply day we rose at 4 A.M. and filled light packs with essential overnight gear and our camp garbage. To lighten our loads, we carried bivvy sacks instead of the tent and left our sleeping bags behind. Instead we elected to sleep in our clothes in the breathable nylon body-length green sacks. With our extra equipment inside the tent, we zipped the door, hoping the wolves would leave everything alone. Although concerned about the safety of our sleeping bags, we risked leaving them, knowing we would return with two spares.

Bill had his doubts about the wisdom of our plan. "I don't trust them," he said, casting a sideways look toward the wolves' den. But my optimistic nature carried the day.

We left camp at 5 A.M., as Alpha and Mother watched closely. We had gone only two hundred feet when Charlie suddenly sat down, faced the den, and howled. All the wolves hurried to join Alpha and Mother while Alpha returned Charlie's howl. The drawn-out, mournful notes filled the meadow with sadness.

To convince Charlie that we would return, we went back to the tent and showed him that our belongings were still inside. But he was adamant. He leaned against the fabric as if to seek its security, and no amount of food bribes would persuade him to leave.

"I never expected him to bond this closely to the wolves," I said. "What should we do? We can't leave him here, alone with the wolves, while we go for the resupply."

With the pack still watching, I stroked Charlie's head and assured him over and over that we would return in a few days.

But he only nudged the tent door, telling us he wanted inside. Bill unzipped the door, and Charlie immediately curled up in his favorite spot, across my sleeping bag. I lay alongside him, quietly explaining why he should leave with us. After another hour, he sat up. When I gently tugged at his leash, he consented to follow us, but after a few feet he turned to face Alpha, who was standing in front of his family and whining softly. Charlie replied with a few yips, then turned to accompany me with his head and tail down.

When Yukon climbs on top of the log, Klondike sees her chance to send her sister off balance.

Suddenly, at the sound of splashing, we turned to see Denali and Beta crossing the stream. They trotted along a thin trail through scattered willows to parallel our course, only two hundred feet away as we hiked down the valley. Once the two wolves set out with us, Charlie stepped in front of Bill and me and strode ahead, tail held high, with a happy, confident spring to his step. He had resumed his role as our leader.

"There must have been some sort of conversation," Bill said as we followed Charlie.

"I'd love to be a wolf for a day, just to figure out what the wolves and Charlie tell each other," I said.

As we trekked toward our meeting place with Margaret, we speculated about Charlie's reluctance to leave. We wondered what would happen in the fall, when we were set to return to our home in the Cascades before beginning our winter journey. Charlie clearly wanted to be with his wolf friends, but although he had tried to prevent us from leaving, he was so completely bonded to Bill and me that he would never have stayed without us. And we would never have left him in the wilderness. Our bond was permanent and inseparable.

We caught fleeting glimpses of the two wolves as they traveled with us down the much shorter route to the Dempster Highway. Although the journey was easier than our route in, and involved no bushwhacking, it still took three eighteen-hour days to reach Margaret, who had parked the truck in an abandoned quarry close to the roadside.

She was disappointed to learn that Charlie's eagerness to return would preclude our camping with her for a few days, as we had originally planned. But she understood Charlie's need to return to the den and our anxiety over the safety of our tent.

Sitting on the tailgate, enjoying enough of a breeze to keep the mosquitoes away, we lunched on peanut butter sandwiches, Charlie's favorite. We regaled Margaret with tales of the wolf family and our many adventures. Denali and Beta were close by but invisible in the surrounding undergrowth.

When we told Margaret of the aerial hunters, she said she had seen the same green plane landing several times at Fort McPherson. "There was a pilot and two American passengers," she told us. "The locals told me the trio hunted wolves and sometimes bear from the air."

While Margaret drove back to Fort McPherson, we trekked with heavy packs up a valley and took another, quicker route we had noticed on our downward journey. We traversed a narrow ravine that cut through a ridge and skirted an enchanting beaver pond, with water gently lapping at its edges, where three adult beavers and two kits watched us cautiously. As we left the pond, we disturbed a moose and calf, who after a startled look splashed away across a bog and disappeared into the willows. The new route led us directly to the den area.

Meanwhile, Denali and Beta continued to parallel our course. As we crested a low pass, I remarked that the wolves must know every square inch of the region and probably wondered on the way down why we were taking the long way. An exuberant Charlie led us at a brisk pace. Even with heavy loads, we took only two days to return due to the much shorter distance and Charlie's energetic pace, fueled by his desire to return to his friends.

Along the way on the edge of a boggy area, we saw a large patch of cotton grass, its white fluffy heads on foot-long stalks in full bloom. Although Charlie bounced with impatience and tugged at his leash when we stopped to pick the delicious roots, we insisted on gathering enough to make a small meal.

An hour from the den, howls of welcome greeted us. In unison, Denali, Beta, and Charlie called back, the tuneful acknowledgment linking the wolf family and our little group. A half mile from the den, Alpha suddenly appeared. With a certain proud majesty to his stride, he led us all home as Denali and Beta followed close on his heels. Charlie, his tail fanning his delight, pulled on his leash, urging us to hurry.

At the den, Mother, the teenagers, and Omega greeted the traveling pack mates and Charlie with tail wagging and yips of pleasure.

But all was not well with our camp. A foot-high hole in one side of the tent, through which a sleeping bag had been dragged into the meadow, was the most obvious damage. The bag had been ripped apart, scattering feathers in all directions. A large hunk lay in a feathery heap just outside the den entrance.

The culprits appeared unconcerned. Once again showing respect for the boundary line, now that we had returned, they were perfectly well mannered, with an air of utter innocence.

We opened the tent door to confront a disaster. Everything lay in a crumpled mess. Charlie, who had already renewed his scent marks, sniffed all around and inside the tent. While we began the task of sorting through the jumbled items, he sat facing the den. In indignant tones, he loudly voiced his protest with hard-edged barks followed by a stern stare-down. The wolves showed no reaction, but we were sure they understood the message.

Considering the rough treatment our neighbors had bestowed upon our belongings and the fact that wolf jaws can crack large moose bones with ease, we were thankful that our gear had survived the ordeal at all. We replaced the ruined sleeping bag with a new one. We could live with the deep teeth marks on the saucepan handle, we quickly decided, and we wouldn't miss the chewed-off corners on the sleeping pads.

The rest of the damage was relatively minor. Three pairs of socks were shredded well beyond further use, and a shirt missed its collar, buttons, and one sleeve. Powerful jaws had crunched a spare compass and two spoons. A pair of sneakers had been reduced to small pieces of fabric, each no larger than a dime. We added a water bottle with the bottom gnawed off to the pile of items committed to the garbage sack. Although we tried to mend the tent as best we could, we finally gave up and unpacked the spare.

My naive notion that the wolves would leave our belongings alone in our absence had certainly been dispelled. Bill was kind enough not to point out how wrong I had been.

After three hours, we had once more returned everything to reasonable order. It took Charlie more time to recover from his indignation. But later he relaxed and appeared to have forgiven the trespassers, as seemed to be the rule here no matter what the disagreement. Neither Charlie nor the wolves harbored grudges.

As the shadows deepened and the sun disappeared beyond the mountains, we cooked a dinner of rice with our precious diced cotton grass roots sprinkled on top. We followed up with hot chocolate and half an apple pie. Margaret had somehow persuaded a local Gwich'in woman of legendary baking fame to make it for us.

It felt good to be back among the wolves.

Escape

A S THE EARLY-MORNING DEW covered Wolf Camp One in a damp blanket, Alpha departed alone, presumably to scent-mark the ridges to the south. An hour later, while Bill was returning from the stream with the clean breakfast dishes, I shook the sleeping bags and spread them over the tent to air.

Suddenly Charlie rose from resting alongside the tent and strained to get as close to the den as his leash would allow. Denali and Beta looked apprehensive too. All three animals gazed intently at a far-off crest to the south. A breeze drifted toward us.

"Are they catching the scent of prey?" Bill wondered aloud.

"Maybe," I answered, "but why are they so anxious?"

Then we heard two short, high-pitched barks. Denali and Omega bolted toward the sound, while the rest of the pack spun to face south. In minutes, an agitated Beta returned and nudged Mother's shoulder as he ushered her into the den. Omega and the teenagers guarded the entrance, watching the ridge. Charlie voiced a warning growl.

"Must be danger close by," Bill said.

Alpha and Denali, shoulder to shoulder, streaked toward the den. Panting, the two disappeared, along with all the other wolves, into the safety of the dugouts or behind boulders.

Charlie, for his part, hid behind a boulder beside the tent and softly barked an alarm. Then we realized: Hunters! We ran to the tent, jerked the aluminum poles out to collapse it, then pulled it and its contents behind Charlie's boulder, crouching there with him.

A long half hour later, he slowly relaxed. The wolves reappeared. Although still vigilant, they seemed less fearful. Alpha and Denali trotted to the ridge but returned in an hour, and the others resumed normal activities.

We re-erected the tent, behind the boulder this time. To ease our concern we hiked to the ridge with Charlie, hoping to detect the cause of the panic. To avoid being seen in case hunters remained in the area, we approached the ridge from the east, scrambling and climbing to the top. Sure that Alpha had detected hunters on his scent-marking tour, we scanned the southern heights with binoculars. A troubled Charlie stared and growled at something far away. At first our human eyes couldn't reach across the distance. Then, just as we were about to give up, we saw two tiny figures on the tundra heading away, the faint outline of rifles slung across their backs.

"I wonder how close they were," Bill said.

"We didn't hear a shot. Perhaps they never saw Alpha," I replied, looking around at the incredibly rough terrain, which could easily conceal a cautious wolf. The men disappeared. Charlie stopped growling.

"Let's see if we can find more signs of hunters," I said as I put the binoculars back in their case.

We swung east around a brutally rugged ridge to follow a shallow valley until it abruptly ended at a sheer wall of loose, gray rock. Two miles from camp, we climbed yet another ridge and found numerous cigarette butts scattered among the footprints of heavy-soled boots. An empty whiskey bottle lay on the ground. The hunters had obviously scouted from the ridge for some time. Looking back over the mountainous landscape between us and the den, we could see why Alpha had most likely been invisible to the hunters.

A chilling wind picked up as we headed back. Storm clouds billowed from the northern horizon. We scrambled as fast as the mountains allowed to avoid being caught in a storm in such hazardous footing.

Three hours later, as the light faded before the approaching storm, we reached camp in time to see Yukon, who had claimed ownership of a golf ball–size rock, being chased by Klondike, who was determined to steal it for herself. Alpha greeted Charlie with a few yips and wagged his tail, while Charlie replied in kind. Ignoring the weather, everyone relaxed. The danger of hunters had passed, and normal life had resumed. Charlie wandered over to the stream for a long drink, then climbed into the tent to sleep.

After checking that all the tent guy lines were secure, Bill and I joined Charlie inside to escape the wind. Dark clouds dipped low over the mountains. Soon torrential rain forced us to zip the door. The wolves quickly forgot their games and found shelter.

Troubled by the idea that hunters, although separated from the den by several craggy ridges, had been actively searching for our wolf friends, Bill and I discussed the day's events as Charlie slept with his head on my lap. We were awed that Charlie and the wolves knew something was wrong even before Alpha sounded the alarm. It had been a clear demonstration of these animals' ability to sense each other's emotions, even when out of sight of each other.

When Beta had shoved Mother into the den and Omega and the teens stood guard at the entrance, it showed us that the wolves were still committed to defending their pups against other human intruders. Even though we had lived close to the family for several weeks, the wolves still had a healthy fear of humans, and when threatened by hunters, they had sought to protect themselves. Because of the alarm the hunters had caused the wolves, we wondered if Mother might delay bringing the pups out of the den. We hoped not. Every time we returned to camp we looked to see if she had perhaps brought them out in our absence.

To the sound of rain and wind, we cooked dinner and slid into our sleeping bags, intent on staying warm while we caught up on our journal notes. But first we had to look for Bill's reading glasses. Such things as gloves, socks, and eyeglasses disappear into the jumbled void of a tent's contents with exasperating frequency, we have found. Even though Bill testily claimed that they had to be in the tent's side pocket, just where he put them, the pocket was empty.

After going through just about everything, I triumphantly found the glasses—squashed but still usable—beneath Charlie, who had watched us placidly during the search but never moved a muscle. Only as a last desperate measure had I slid my hand beneath his heavy body. "Charlie, you knew they were there all the time!" Bill exclaimed.

While Charlie did not reply to Bill, at least not in this particular instance, he frequently expressed himself to the wolves with howls, yips, and tail wagging. When an energetic activity was in progress near the den, Charlie usually became an interested bystander. But after his first try, with the teens, met with no invitation, he never again attempted to join the activities. Instead he often initiated his own game of chase with Bill and me, just as he often did at home, as if to show the pack, which always stopped to watch.

Whenever he indicated to us that it was time for a game, we let him off his leash to allow him room to maneuver. He would race away then turn to head straight at us, dodging at the last moment, racing around the tent and heading for us again, barely avoiding our outstretched hands. It was impossible to catch him. Sometimes Bill tried to outwit Charlie by diving headfirst to cut him off, but it was my husband who always ended up sprawled on the ground, with Charlie making another daring pass.

*Cautious Mother watches us with suspicion
and keeps her pups hidden.*

The wolves' response was one of intense curiosity as they gathered to watch the spectacle. Once Charlie discovered he had an attentive audience, he was spurred to new heights of ambush. He hid behind the boulder beside our tent, and when we pretended we didn't know he was there and walked by, he leaped out, racing past us at full throttle. When exhaustion ended the game, we clipped Charlie's leash back on. He usually got a drink of water and then slept hard, just as the wolves did following a strenuous game.

At times Charlie made it clear that he wanted to be free of his leash. But he generally accepted it, as if he understood that we could not allow him to roam freely among the wolves. In our adventure, his safety came above all else.

One day, though, we were tempted to take the risk. The three of us were hiking through a secluded valley of willow and spruce a little west of the den, scouting the slopes above for Dall sheep. It was midafternoon, and after seeing a group of eight sheep and lambs who looked down at us with only mild interest, we were about to return to camp when Charlie barked to be let off his leash. We guessed that he wanted closer contact with the sheep.

At first I was adamant that we not break our rule of keeping him secured to the leash at all times, except when playing with us in camp. But as his pleading intensified and the sheep wandered out of sight, I began to consider letting him off just this once, thinking he would lead us back to camp. He wouldn't chase after the sheep now that he couldn't see them, I reasoned.

Bill agreed, sure that Charlie would stay close to us. But the moment he was free, he ran partway up the slope and at full speed followed the rocky trail the sheep had taken. He was soon out of sight in spite of our calls.

We stumbled across the uneven ground and up the slope to the narrow trail, hurrying as fast as the terrain allowed, which was nowhere near the speed at which Charlie had traveled. By now we were yelling at the top of our lungs, frantically trying to persuade him to return. We rounded a turn in the trail just in time to see him disappear as he chased the sheep over the next ridge. We quickly crested the ridge, but there was no sign of Charlie or the sheep.

We were distraught. We climbed down into the next valley, unsure which direction Charlie had taken. An hour went by with no sign of him. With tears streaming down my face, I followed Bill until he finally stopped and turned to face me. "We're never going to find him in such a rugged wilderness," he said.

But we kept calling him anyway, with voices that were almost hoarse, and talked about where to turn next. I was reluctant to return to the den, but Bill argued that Charlie knew where the den was, and unless he ran into trouble with strange wolves, he would return. We sadly turned back. Bill put his arm around my shoulders, trying to convince me that Charlie was okay. But his words sounded hollow, and I was inconsolable.

As we walked back, we kept calling. In an hour we reached the outskirts of the den area, at which point we became quiet lest our uncustomary loud voices disturb the wolves, who were lounging around the den. I was so upset that I hardly glanced at the teens and Beta, who lay close to Charlie's scent-marked boundary. Bill was glum and silent.

Suddenly a large black form crested the ridge above us and there was Charlie, calmly trotting downward to meet us with no sign of fatigue. We rushed him. I hugged him tight while Bill stroked his back. We were so giddy with relief we couldn't be angry. I cried tears of joy. Then Charlie calmly led us back to the tent and set about the serious business of licking his paws clean, while Bill clicked his leash firmly in place.

Although his calm return reminded us that Charlie was perfectly capable of taking care of himself, we knew we had broken an important wilderness rule. Many times, as we hiked in the Cascade Range, we had encountered hikers frantically searching for a lost dog. Often, in spite of trail rules that require dogs to remain on leashes, an owner releases a pet with the misguided notion that the animal will be happier. Many such animals, attracted by a wild scent, leave the trail and are never found; they fall victim to coyotes roaming the mountains. Now we understood the panic of those pet owners.

In relief, we sat outside the tent, sharing peanuts and allowing our nerves to settle, while Charlie begged for food until we filled his bowl. We wondered just how far had he chased the sheep and whether he had heard us calling him. But all that really mattered was that he was with us again.

Pups

CLEAR SKY THE NEXT MORNING heralded a glorious sunny day. All the wolves except Mother left to hunt. When they returned three hours later, Alpha carried the leg of an adult moose. Denali and Omega followed, each dragging portions that were so heavy they had to straddle the precious meat with their front legs. The teenagers followed, accompanied by Beta, the wise old wolf, who appeared to urge the young ones on as they struggled with bulky loads. Beta carried nothing. We assumed his job was to supervise the teenagers, who hunted with increasing frequency as the summer progressed.

The moose carcass was a bloody, grisly sight. Most of the skin had been torn off, and the head was missing. The hunters' bellies were distended with food they had eaten at the kill site. Once at the den, Alpha left his load for Mother, and the rest left theirs in the shade. After Mother ate her fill and drank from the stream, she returned to the den while the rest of the pack relaxed and slept. Three hours later they all rose and gorged themselves again.

Around midnight, Denali and Alpha trotted away. They returned around 2 A.M. with an uneaten hare and a partly devoured beaver, which they left close to the den entrance. Mother came out and sat down alone to enjoy the bounty at her door. Apparently unable to eat much more, she left most of the beaver for the two teenagers, whose hostility as they competed for the food was at first subtle, then more serious as the beaver disappeared. They snarled at each other while gulping the last pieces. Part of the beaver's furry skin served in a tug-of-war game the next day.

Now we knew that the wolves sometimes caught beavers. The sight of the limp beaver's body saddened us. We hoped it was not from the marsh we had visited.

We awoke early the next morning to the sound of snarling and crunching. The pack, including Mother, was devouring the rest of the moose. Omega darted back and forth, snatching meat whenever the opportunity presented itself. He appeared to have perfected the art of stealth. Sometimes a neighbor growled into his face as he grabbed a piece, but his quickness allowed him to escape with his prize intact.

After observing the activities for most of the night, we returned to our sleeping bags. The sound of wolves yipping happily awoke us. We forced our reluctant, sleep-deprived bodies from the tent to see what was going on in the neighborhood.

What we saw made us promptly forget our lack of sleep. Before us was the sight we had been longing for: Mother had two pups out on full display.

Their short, round bodies were covered in fluffy gray fur. They stood on stubby legs with feet that appeared far too large. Their little ears pointed upward, their tails were short and thin, and their eyes were still blue. It was the second week of June, so the pups must have been four weeks old. Alpha nudged them toward the stream. They clearly had no desire to go anywhere near the water. They wobbled back to Mother on unsteady legs, only to have her push them toward the water again. But the pups had made up their minds: They were not going close to the stream, at least not today.

Charlie was fascinated. He made gentle whimpering sounds and wagged his tail as he bounded to the end of his leash to meet the pups. Given their feeble eyesight at this age, they at first didn't see him. Then one round furball looked up, paused a moment to figure out what Charlie was, then tottered toward

The sight we long for: Mother brings her two pups out of the den.

him. We started toward Charlie to lead him away from the pup in case Mother and her kin became upset. But before we could reach him, he had already bent to nuzzle the new wolf.

We stopped in midstride. The meeting was going well, and the adults didn't seem distressed. Mother walked slowly toward Charlie and stopped fifteen feet away. Charlie saw her and nosed the pup in her direction. The little fellow adjusted his eyes, saw his mother, and wove his way back to her as fast as his short legs would take him. He immediately reached for a nipple and had a milk break. Then Mother returned the pups to the den while the rest of the family stretched out in the shade. As for Bill and me, we were overjoyed to have finally seen the pups. Until now we had worried that Mother would be too nervous to allow her pups so close to us.

Wolves are born blind and deaf. They can hear a week after birth, but their eyes don't open for two weeks, and even then they don't see well. Over the next few weeks their eyesight improves. We suspected that Mother had taken the pups out of the den now and then over the previous week, while we were away from our camp, but had been uncertain of our trustworthiness until now. Apparently we had gained her confidence.

The gestation period for wolves is sixty to sixty-three days. This small litter was far below the average of six pups. Mothers have eight teats, so a small litter of only two would receive plenty of milk, eliminating the competition that results from larger litters.

Mother usually stayed inside until late afternoon. Just as we began to cook dinner that night, a pup appeared outside the den and was quickly joined by his brother. They inspected a small pebble, rolling it around and pushing it with their blunt noses. Suddenly their attention shifted to a raven's black feather on the ground. A battle ensued over who would keep the feather. After a short tussle, one tried to run off with his prize, while the other pursued him on his short new legs. They both collided with a high rock and promptly sat down.

The teenagers, who appeared to have pup-sitting responsibilities, nudged both little ones back to the den. For the next week, the pups were not allowed to wander more than a few feet. Beta kept an eye on both the pups and the teenagers, but Bill and I suspected he was mostly watching to make sure the teenagers performed their pup-sitting duties adequately.

As the days passed, the pups spent more time out of the den and were allowed to investigate some enticing rocks a few yards away. They were the center of the family's attention. While Mother, the teenagers, and Beta spent the most time with them, the rest of the pack was attentive as well. Even Omega nuzzled them without incurring any wrath.

One sunny June afternoon, Bill and I had stretched out on our sleeping pads to enjoy a snooze in the meadow, wolf-style. The mosquitoes, disliking the breeze, had left us in peace. The only sound was the gurgle of the nearby stream. Charlie lay close to his scent-marked boundary, dreaming the afternoon away. The wolves dozed in favorite places.

Suddenly Charlie broke the quiet with soft yipping. We awoke to see a pup pulling Charlie's fur, begging him to play. As Charlie got to his feet, he ever so gently nosed the pup toward Mother, who rested alongside the den. At the sound of Charlie's yips, she and the others awoke. Charlie returned the pup as far as his boundary, where he was met by Alpha.

We half-expected trouble, but Charlie had won the pack's trust, even with their most precious possession. Alpha calmly herded the pup the rest of the way to the den. Then, with the pup returned to Mother, everyone, including Charlie, went back to sleep.

Each day the pups expanded their perimeter as they grew stronger. They cautiously approached the stream and tested it with inquisitive black noses, then jumped back in alarm when the water splashed their faces. Mother, always close by, ushered them away whenever they were in any danger of falling in. As the pups grew older, the two teenagers spent more time with them, even engaging in gentle games of tug-of-war.

Mother left the pups in the care of Yukon and Klondike one day while she hunted with the pack. The two pup-sitters lay in the sun as the youngsters climbed all over them. Even when the pups braced their short legs and pulled Yukon's fur ruff as hard as they could, she endured without protest. Only when the pups grabbed Klondike's irresistible tail and pulled and shook it, as if to separate the whole thing from its owner, did Klondike halt the game.

But it was a momentary interruption. Klondike's ear was too tempting and became the next "toy." Needle teeth bit hard, causing Klondike to growl an indignant protest as she jumped to her feet. Swatting the offending pup with a front paw, she sent him tumbling head over heels. The pup staggered to his feet, reoriented himself, and charged back to grab another mouthful of fur.

Their short rounded bodies are covered in fluffy gray fur.

Klondike and Yukon displayed remarkable patience, but they eventually tired of fur pulling and switched to chase. The little gray balls on short legs weren't fast enough. Soon they found they could catch their victim if they waited for the quarry to return. At just the right moment, they would leap, grab a pup-sitter, and hang on, their bodies dragging for a few feet until they let go. The game continued until both pups lay exhausted. Klondike and Yukon stretched out alongside them, and all slept. An occasional swat at an offending mosquito was the only movement.

July's first week had arrived. We sat in the shade beside the tent, catching up on our journal entries and sorting camera film. A brisk breeze kept the mosquitoes away. Charlie dozed close to the stream. Suddenly the ponderous sound of a large animal fighting through willows farther downstream caught our attention. Jumping to our feet, Bill and I grabbed our loaded shotguns and waited with taut nerves as the crashing sounds moved closer. Charlie stood growling in anticipation, while the wolves sounded short barks of warning. The teenagers and Mother watched from the den entrance with the pups tucked away inside.

Moments later an adult cinnamon-colored grizzly, easily identified by the massive muscled hump that lay across his shoulders, burst through the undergrowth and marched toward Charlie, his mouth agape and his huge, square head swinging back and forth on powerful shoulders. Charlie's snarls increased through bared teeth as he leaped at the bear at the end of his long leash, only fifty feet from the aggressive intruder. The wolves, led by Alpha with hackles raised in anger on the far side of the stream, sped toward the grizzly. The bear quickly turned his thick head toward the pack and tore into the stream to attack.

Charlie again leaped high in the air with an ear-tingling, mouth-frothing snarl. The bear momentarily turned to fix his black eyes on Charlie's furious defense, then spun to race back downstream, clearly impressed by Charlie's savage appearance. The wolves instantly gave chase to the fast-retreating bear, who fled to the safety of open space where he wouldn't be trapped by willows. The pack dashed at top speed across the tundra to disappear over a low rise, leaving us staring into the silence. Charlie remained on guard until the wolves and bear disappeared.

Later, as evening mountain shadows crossed the valley, the pack trotted back single-file to the den. Charlie interrupted his dinner to stand on his side of the stream as the wolves greeted him with happy tail wagging. With the pack on one side of the stream and Charlie on the other, they joined in a chorus, heads back, howling to the sky. Charlie's voice, of a similar pitch, spiraled up and down the scale with the wild voices.

In minutes the howling session ceased. The wolves continued to the den, where the pups rushed to greet them. Charlie returned to his dinner, but later that night he walked to the willows from which the bear had charged and carefully scent-marked all along the edge of the tangled thicket, perhaps as a warning to any other bear who might approach. Discussing the day's events before bedtime, Bill and I surmised that the bear's sensitive nose had detected the odor of leftover moose bones and meat scraps around the den.

The wolf family often enjoyed a good community howl. They celebrated joyfully when happy, and when returning from a hunt. Often a hunting party signaled their return long before their arrival by howling across the tundra or from a distant ridge. The echo would hardly have faded before the wolves at home replied with cries of joy.

Sometimes one wolf would simply start howling for no apparent reason, and the rest would join the songfest. Occasionally, after a long sleep, one wolf would wake up and begin a sleepy howl. Others would awaken and join in as if the activity were meant to clear their heads. These choruses began slowly and built as all the wolves became fully alert. Each wolf always sang in his own key and changed keys at will, causing two or three wolves to sound like a large pack.

Omega, the underdog, would sometimes be disciplined after tentatively joining a session. Alpha or Beta would stand over him as he groveled on his back. Eventually he would be allowed to slink away and howl from a distance. But most of the time he boldly joined in without incurring any discipline. It appeared that his skill lay in judging when to join the group and when to quietly stay in the background.

Although we knew that Omega's role filled the family's need for an occasional scapegoat, we found ourselves reflexively taking his side during confrontations. It was hard to watch him groveling for forgiveness when there appeared to have been no real infraction of the rules. As a result, our fondness for him grew beyond the close affection for the rest of the family that we steadily developed over our months in the wilderness.

The wolves' strong social nature enabled them to form lasting emotional attachments with other pack members. The pups, profoundly attached to everyone, expressed absolute delight with excited bounces and frisky play when an adult played with them. They were especially bonded to Mother and Beta, and when either animal left to hunt, the pups gave them a wild welcome upon their return.

The adults often returned from scent-marking or hunting with a new stick or even a rock, which they lay outside the den, ready for the next frolic. Hunting, eating, playing, and sleeping were the major daily activities. After an abundant feast they frequently slept for six or seven hours.

The pups were often a nuisance to sleeping adults. They slept long hours themselves, after which they attempted to play with any pack member within reach, regardless of whether he or she was in the mood. Their supply of energy and stamina seemed endless. Although the pups often tested the other wolves' patience, if the victims were too groggy to play, they just moved to another spot without visible protest. If the pup persisted, we sometimes heard a soft warning growl. Usually the pups took the hint.

Most of their games involved play-fighting. They pinned each other's necks and growled and attacked again and again. One day they battled each other so vigorously that they rolled into the stream. Although this play helped build quick, strong bodies, it also prepared them for traveling long distances to find prey. Play-fighting also developed their competitive spirit, crucial to the establishment of their social rank as they matured.

Sometimes play became too serious, though. Often the brothers assaulted each other as if to tear limb from limb. As sharp teeth sank into soft flesh, their loud protests of outrage induced them to fight each other with even more murderous intent. At this point another wolf, often Beta or one of the teenagers, would put a stop to the free-for-all and demand peace in puppyville.

Eating was a mad, unrestrained ritual. At first the pups suckled at Mother's teats, but as they grew they consumed an increasing amount of meat, first eating only food partly predigested by the other wolves. Whenever a hunting party returned with food, the pups swarmed the adults, frantically whining and licking their muzzles, which stimulated the adults to regurgitate partly digested meat. In a frenzy, the pups snatched the food almost before it hit the ground. Every scrap disappeared in seconds. We soon realized the origin of the expression "He wolfed his food down."

The youngsters usually chose Beta or Alpha first, having learned these two usually provided food for them. The rest of the adults also provided nourishment at various times, but in smaller amounts. Sometimes a wolf regurgitated only part of its supply. Beta was particularly fussy. He would initially give a cup-size pile, then continue in several places, and finally stand back to watch the pups rapidly consume their fill.

After weaning at about eight weeks, the pups continued to eat regurgitated meat, but gradually consumed more fresh food. When the hunters dropped a carcass at the den, the pups leaped in with uninhibited gusto to feed alongside the adults, who always allowed the pups to eat until they could hold no more.

The hunters continually returned with an ample supply of prey in their jaws. Alpha, who often carried meat back to the den, always left his supply in one large heap. Later, even Yukon and Klondike, as they matured as hunters, supplied food. The entire family took responsibility for feeding and raising their cherished offspring. We never saw any wolf attempt to steal the pups' food.

As the pups' legs grew longer and stronger, they frequently climbed the ridge. Normally an adult accompanied them, usually Yukon, Klondike, Beta, or Mother. If they wandered off alone, a pack member instantly nudged them to head back. One day Beta herded a pup all the way back from the top, pushing the pup's rear with his nose. At other times, a pup-sitter might lift the pup in gentle jaws and carry him home.

The whole family enjoyed high places, not only to watch for prey but also to lounge and dreamily gaze into the distance. They all loved exploring the nooks and crannies, which were perfect for ambushing a pack mate.

One afternoon a game unfolded as Yukon crouched and hid on the ridge top. Just as an unwary Klondike arrived, Yukon leaped at her unsuspecting sister. In the ensuing wrestling match, the pair rolled in a tight embrace all the way to the bottom. Occasionally, both wolves ganged up on an older member, and all three would tussle until too tired to continue.

As summer progressed, the mosquitoes attacked in bloodsucking hordes, rushing to complete their life cycle. If there was even a hint of a breeze, the wolves climbed to the crest of the windiest spot to escape the black swarms. Mother at first coped by retreating to the den with the pups, but as they grew, she would take them to a nearby windy ridge to relax in peace. We soon learned to follow their example when our sheltered valley became unbearable under a haze of the pests. We also wore netting over our hats and faces, and liberally spread deet over the fabric of our shirts.

The breeze not only kept mosquitoes away but also provided information concerning prey in the area. The wolves spent long hours sniffing with raised snouts for the special scent that revealed prey within range. When a promising odor was detected, they would assemble a hunting party and leave to stalk the prey. A wolf's sense of smell is so acute that it can detect a scent many miles away, and its eyesight and hearing are just as impressive. Such highly tuned senses enable the pack to locate prey efficiently with the least amount of energy expenditure, a valuable trait for a predator in a land where food is sometimes scarce.

Early one morning as I prepared breakfast, Mother vigorously enlarged an old dugout a hundred feet from the den. She then carried the pups one at a time to the mound, probably hoping both would stay there while she worked. In minutes they ran in opposite directions. Mother stopped digging, hurrying to bring one back from the stream and the other from the ridge. But by the time she returned with the second pup, the first had already disappeared.

She let out a series of irritated yips. The two teenagers ran to her side. After a brief nuzzle with Mother, they set off after the troublemakers and soon ushered them back to the den, where Yukon and Klondike pup-sat while Mother finished her work in peace. A game of chase followed by a wrestling match kept the pups entertained.

Meanwhile, as Mother continued her task with the efficiency of a backhoe, the space quickly grew to twice its original size. The teenagers and their charges wandered over to inspect Mother's work. After considerable sniffing all around the five-foot-wide entrance, the two pups attempted a little practice digging and then went inside to investigate. They apparently approved of the new accommodations, because an hour elapsed before they emerged.

Later Alpha and Denali, who had been out hunting, returned with a hare and inspected the enlarged dugout, after which they expressed their satisfaction by initiating a howling session. The entire family and Charlie joined in.

At first the pups simply watched; then, with pursed lips raised to the sky, they added wavering voices. The adults stopped and stared. Then, as if in celebration of the youngsters' first attempts, they all howled together. The various pitches of the mature adults contrasted with the reedy, thin tones of the pups. As the last note died on the breeze, the adults nuzzled the pups affectionately and licked their faces.

Neighbors

I N MID-JULY, when the pups were about eight weeks old, Mother moved them from the den to the dugout, where they stayed from then on while the adults hunted. At this "rendezvous site," the fast-growing youngsters moved about more freely, went on walks of increasing length with Beta or sometimes Mother, and learned how to catch small animals such as lemmings. When not eating or sleeping, they played ever more vigorous games as they grew. They would never again enter the den.

The term "rendezvous site," still used today, was coined by pioneering wolf biologist Adolph Murie. Beginning in 1939, he studied wolf behavior in the region that would later become Denali National Park. There he noticed that when a pack transferred young from the den, they established several spots that provided not only more room but also greater security. The pups, who required larger feedings as they grew, remained alone when the pack spent longer hours away. When the hunters returned with food, they met and fed the youngsters at these rendezvous sites.

Wolves sometimes move pups a mile or more away, so we were relieved that the family hadn't gone too far from our campsite. The new home, only two hundred feet from the den, allowed us to continue our close observation of the family. While exploring the surrounding ridges and valleys, we found several places with trampled and packed earth that appeared to have been used in past years as rendezvous sites, probably by this pack. We assumed that sites close by had been chosen because the area was so secure, especially from aircraft. Also, this location was surrounded by a plentiful supply of game.

By now the teenagers were as large as the adults, their bodies filled out and muscular. Mother, Yukon, and Klondike participated in almost every hunt, which left Beta to care for and teach the pups most of the time. When at the den, though, Mother spent her time with her young. Even after several hours on a hunt, she stayed close to the pups upon her return and often took them for short walks, usually along the main trail.

Two days after the youngsters moved to their new home, all the adults except Beta left at 3 A.M. to hunt. Beta gathered his charges and set out through the trees on a simpler expedition. We followed at a distance so as not to distract the pups and earn Beta's displeasure. For every hundred feet Beta traveled, the pups scurried, swerved, and darted at least three times as far, as they plunged inquisitive noses into clumps of grasses and sedges. They sniffed everything; they picked up sticks and then dropped them when other, more inviting specimens took their place.

One pup suddenly galloped full speed into the trees. With a reprimanding yip, Beta ran to the pup, picked him up around his middle, and dumped him roughly back on the trail. The subdued brothers quietly went along for a few yards but soon resumed their darting, circling travel pattern.

When Beta turned to go back to the rendezvous site, we waited quietly in the trees until the entourage passed. We were unnoticed by the pups, who were too busy exploring the new sights and sounds of their rapidly enlarging world.

One evening while on a jaunt with the pups, Beta spied a lemming as it scurried for safety. He pounced and held the little body down while the youngsters sprang to sniff it. Beta crunched the still body, killing it, then left it. The pups vigorously leaped on it, shook it, and chewed it. They "killed" it again and again, until Beta reached over, grabbed it in his mouth, and swallowed. The game was finished. The pups had just completed their first hunting lesson.

As summer progressed, their bodies gradually lost their "baby" look. The pups attempted to explore by themselves, but a pack mate always returned them to the site. Still strictly supervised, the brothers were not allowed to wander. These pups were the pack's most precious possessions, and were still too young to defend themselves against predators.

Steady fifteen-mile-per-hour winds swept the ridges in the last few days of July, carrying the scent of prey to the wolves standing watch from the ridge top. The pack usually hunted every day, but occasionally they would miss a day or two, especially after they killed a large animal such as a moose.

Watching the pack drag home the remains of a moose reminded us of the danger inherent in what these smaller predators must do to survive. Although wolves possess daring and fast reaction time, one swipe of a moose hoof can crack a wolf's jaw or skull. A broken jaw easily renders a wolf incapable of hunting and eating, thus possibly dooming it to a slow and agonizing death.

One day Beta returned after an apparently unsuccessful family hunt, limping heavily on a cut right front paw. He lay at the rendezvous site licking the wound. The rest of the family gathered around him. After Klondike watched closely for a few minutes, she nudged Beta's muzzle and then licked the wound. Mother caressed Beta's face with long, tender strokes. Yukon took the pups off to play close to the old den, probably to prevent them from mobbing Beta. Denali, who usually showed the least emotion of all the wolves (except around the time of a hunt), sat beside Beta and whimpered sympathetically. It was an astonishing moment: wolves seeming to act exactly like humans.

A few minutes later, Klondike stopped licking her pack mate's wound. Beta stood and walked a few steps, but the injury

The scent of prey carries to the wolves, who watch from the ridgetop.

was too painful and he lay down again. We wondered if he had been kicked when charging a large animal. For the rest of the day, the family stayed close to him. We were moved by the genuine caring the wolves displayed which contrasted sharply with their reputation as ruthless killers.

The dignified Beta always acted as if respect for his seniority was his to enjoy without question. During the next week he stayed home sunning himself or sleeping in the shade while the pack hunted. The teenagers kept the pups occupied.

Only once did the pups attempt to tease Beta into playing. At his first annoyed yip, Klondike raced to his side and escorted the mischievous brothers away for a game of chase. They raced back and forth, swerving and dodging through the nearby trees until both teen and pups collapsed from their exertion.

After each successful hunt, one of the hunters, usually Denali or Omega, placed food before Beta. Omega even dropped his shy cloak to sit beside Beta while he ate, as if to make sure the meal was sufficient for his superior.

That night after dinner, as Bill and I reflected on Beta's injury and the pack's strong family ties and loyalty, I realized that the wolves had become a vital part of our existence. Their unfailing devotion to each other had flowed into our own lives to make us pause and consider our human attitudes. In the quiet of the valleys and mountains surrounding us, it was easy to think and care like a wolf and to at least begin to see life as they saw it. In the far-off bustle of our other life, would we lose some of what we had learned from these wolves?

"We've learned more from these animals than we ever expected," Bill said. "Wise old Beta has a lot to teach us."

Beta stopped limping after a week of rest and appeared to have recovered. We were relieved: A permanently injured wolf has little chance of survival, especially in a climate that demands aggressive hunting in winters so harsh that even many healthy animals live on the brink. Beta occasionally rejoined the hunts, but as summer progressed he spent most of his days teaching, escorting, and watching the pups.

The first crisp days of August brought a frosty sparkle of autumn to signal the end of mosquito season. Early-morning breezes chilled the tips of our noses while our fingers sought the warm comfort of gloves. The twenty-four hours of daylight were fading into increasing hours of darkness, and daily temperatures hovered in the 30s. Yellow and red glowed through the summer green of willows and tundra plants. The wolves' coats visibly thickened as they prepared to meet the bitter cold of a long, dark winter. All the birds disappeared, leaving to spend winter in warmer climates, except for the exasperating ravens.

By now we had considerably deepened our appreciation of the wolves' distinct personalities. Mother, elegant and feminine, remained the most impatient member of the family. She was the boss and strict disciplinarian. Even Alpha dared not cross her, especially when the pups were very young and she spent most of her time with them at the den. But although sometimes sharp with the adults, Mother was always tender and patient with the pups. She frequently licked each one from head to tail until satisfied they were clean.

After the pups moved to the rendezvous site, though, she hunted more frequently and visibly mellowed. She still scolded the teenagers when they wrestled too close to her or if they had the brashness to step forward and attempt to eat before she did. The teens soon learned to behave in her presence when her mood turned dark.

Cleanliness was important to Mother. A fastidious groomer, she spent more time cleaning her paws in the stream after a meal than any other wolf. She even dunked her head into the water to remove any trace of blood from her jaws and face.

Dominant Alpha demanded respect from everyone except Mother, for whom his adoration never waned. Although as family head Alpha was respected, his was not a harsh rule. While his authority was firm, he was also the biggest clown at game time.

When the pups were confined to the den immediately after birth, Alpha took food to Mother. He later left an abundant supply outside the entrance just for her. No matter how mouth-watering the morsels might have seemed to the other wolves, Alpha's stern countenance persuaded others never to touch her food. Whenever she emerged from the den to eat and to clean herself, Alpha stood watch, as if basking in her approval of the meal he had provided. The only time he relinquished leadership of the pack was during a hunt, when he passed the role to Denali.

Denali led the hunts with unwavering authority, always the first to charge prey. His athletic form flowed across the unstable tundra mounds with the grace of a ballet dancer. When he leaped on small prey, it was with a natural elegance enhanced by his long, sleek body and luxurious coat. He spent much of his time on the nearby ridges watching for prey. When he gathered the group before a hunt, he ran to each of the wolves in turn, licking their muzzles as if to inspire them. He often displayed allegiance to Alpha before a hunt by gently rubbing against Alpha's shoulder with his own. Then Denali would set off with head and ears thrust forward, leading the rest.

When not hunting, Denali blended into the pack as a mellow member. On hot days, not only would he lie in the stream shallows with the other wolves, but he would often go one step further and roll in the water.

Beta, an experienced senior, disciplined the teenagers whenever they disobeyed rules. He never allowed them to disrespect others, and when their play became too rough, he always stepped in to call a halt. He would stand over them and force them to grovel on their backs, then walk away. Until he returned to signal them to rise, they would remain motionless on the ground. They resumed play only after confirming that Beta had forgiven them.

If the pups strayed, Beta would either carry them home or usher them back by pushing them on their little gray rears. In the spring he had often taken Yukon and Klondike on short hunts, but as they matured and joined the adults, he devoted his full attention to the pups' schooling.

Omega still remained on the edge of the pack, but now he often joined games. He played gently and was as quick as lightning as he darted and spun, leaving playmates grasping at air. Although always the last to eat, he became bolder as the summer progressed. His role of scapegoat became less of a burden. He no longer automatically cowered submissively when a superior approached, although he continued to display caution around Alpha, who occasionally nipped him when he approached too soon at mealtimes. We wondered if he kept to the edge of family life and had taken on the role of omega due to his shyness. He took longer than the rest to fully accept Charlie, and even longer to accept Bill and me. But by August, he had dropped his suspicion of us.

Even though the rapidly maturing teens' hunting responsibilities had increased over the summer, Klondike and Yukon remained high-spirited and full of fun and energy, always looking for a game. When they tired of teasing each other, they went in search of an adult who was willing to play chase. A favorite joke on a hot day was to race at top speed through the stream just as another wolf bent to drink. The thoroughly doused victim often joined them. After they had spent the last of their energy, they flopped down to enjoy the cool water.

When not hunting, the teens at first joined Beta in pup-sitting chores. They not only played with the brothers but also kept them close to the den. Later, after the pups moved to the rendezvous site, Beta sometimes rested from his teaching duties. Then the teens accompanied the pups on short sojourns through the spruce trees to a meadow flanked by sheer rock walls, where a few noisy ravens nested in crevices. An abundant lemming population lived in burrows beneath this carpet of moss, which would become a perfect place for the young wolves to learn to hunt.

The pups displayed separate temperaments as they matured. One was clearly more dominant, even to the extent of sometimes baring tiny white teeth in his fiercest growl, while his brother was the clown, racing around in blissful happiness.

As they grew, their boldness reached impressive levels. They stalked Klondike and Yukon and, at just the right moment, pounced and grabbed the teens' tails and pulled as if to separate each tail from its owner. One midday a little brother climbed onto Yukon's reclining body, with the end of the teen's tail firmly clasped in his sharp teeth, to gain extra leverage from the higher vantage point. His sibling raced to help, and with both standing on top of poor Yukon pulling with all their might, it wasn't long before she rose with a yelp of protest. The gray bundles slid to the ground in a heap.

Sometimes a pup attacked an adult's tail while his brother grabbed the ears. We marveled that the teenagers and Beta retained any ears at all. The pup-sitters regained peace only when they swatted the offenders as a reminder that even babies must follow the rules. The destruction of tails and ears was forbidden.

The pups were a great source of entertainment for us. Often, after eating their fill of fresh meat, they played on top of the food, much to the annoyance of the adults still eating. A growl and a firm swat usually removed them from the dinner table. When a pup buried something to keep as his own there was invariably an indignant yowl of protest from the owner when his brother discovered the treasure and stole it.

Charlie did not escape the pups' play. He watched them with his soft gaze and, with enticing yips, occasionally invited them to visit when he sat close to his boundary. While still very

A favorite game is to race full speed through the stream,
dousing playmates along the way.

young, they would wobble over and pull his tail. As they grew, they climbed on his prone body and wrestled with his thick wolflike fur. Then one day they found his ear. As tiny teeth clamped down, Charlie suddenly jerked his head upward, dumping one pup on the ground. Charlie instantly reached out to pin the offender with a large paw. His sibling slid off Charlie's back, landed within reach of Charlie's other paw, and found himself pinned just like his brother. Charlie allowed them to break free only after considerable squirming. They swung to attack again, but Charlie decided that it was time for the game to end. He stood and sounded two yips that brought Mother and Beta on the run. They each picked up a pup and carried him home.

We were delighted to see that the wolves didn't mind Charlie's occasional interaction with the pups. They apparently sensed that their offspring were safe with him.

As the pups grew, their eyesight improved. They would stare across to where they thought Charlie should be, then make a beeline for him. One afternoon he took them to the stream to join him in a drink. But instead of lapping the water they tried to nuzzle Charlie, apparently assuming that he would provide them with water from his mouth, the same way the adults regurgitated meat for them. Charlie, no doubt puzzled, ignored their odd behavior and kept on lapping until they got the hint. The pups enjoyed playing in the water, leaping at the ripples that flowed by, although they made no attempt to explore farther downstream among the willows, where the grizzly had emerged weeks before.

Most of the time Charlie was content to watch the pups' antics from a distance. After they lost their baby habits, he no longer invited them to play. When they approached his boundary, he informed them with a soft but authoritative growl that he preferred that they observe his property rights. They were quick to learn his limits and stay back. We were also concerned that if they spent too much time in Charlie's territory, our relationship with their family might be impaired, so we often shooed them back home. By the time the pups moved to the rendezvous site, they were staying in their own territory exclusively. All the wolves respected Charlie's scent marks. After we caught the adults snooping around the tent, they crossed the invisible line only sporadically, usually just to run across a corner to inspect the tiny movement of a lemming, which of course demanded instant attention.

As we became more familiar with the wolves, we also grew more adept at recognizing their various facial expressions. The wolves' normal expression was relaxed, except when they submitted to a higher-ranking wolf. Then they groveled, held their heads low, flattened their ears, and turned their lips downward. At times they offered an apologetic paw from a turned-away body. When angry they pulled their lips back into a snarl and wrinkled their muzzles, displaying long white fangs. At playtime they smiled, with lips pulled back and slightly turned up at the corners.

Differences were often settled with snarls or sharp nips on shoulders or rumps. Occasionally, a wolf of a higher rank pinned and stood over a subservient member after some transgression, such as an attempt to eat out of turn. The teens and pups, although often disciplined for misbehavior, were never injured. We never observed a serious adult fight that ended in injury. Even pack scapegoat Omega, although sometimes picked on and cowed, was never harmed.

One evening after watching from our usual lookout ridge above the junction, we took a shortcut to where the wolves appeared headed for a hunt. But we chose the wrong route and were soon left far behind. Giving up, we explored a new ridge and then returned to camp, where we found that Yukon and Klondike, who had remained at the rendezvous site with the pups, had scattered a carton of breakfast cereal that we had purposely left outside the tent as a test. Of course, when we appeared, both wolves sat innocently paying attention to the pups. Yukon walked a few steps toward us as if curious to know whether we noticed the mess, but scurried away when we looked in her direction.

A mortified Charlie sniffed the area. Then he strode resolutely to his scent marks and proceeded to slowly and deliberately refresh his posts with frequent resentful glances toward the young neighbors. They slumped with heads on paws, eyes averted from Charlie's wrathful stare. For a half hour he silently punished them, but then dinnertime arrived. The moment Charlie went inside our tent for his meal, the two young wolves

visibly relaxed and rose to their feet. Perhaps they heaved a collective sigh of relief that at last they were forgiven. They never disturbed our tent or belongings again.

Charlie often sits close to his scent boundary and watches the pups with his soft gaze.

Early one sunny mid-August morning, in temperatures that hovered around freezing, we headed out to follow Denali, who led Alpha, Mother, and Omega on a hunt. The foursome loped along at a good pace, generally avoiding getting sidetracked by interesting things along the trail.

On the tundra, two female moose with two large calves grazed in the distance. One mother raised her head and saw the wolves, and then all four bolted to the north at a fast pace, quickly disappearing into the safety of a distant valley. The wolves stopped, as if to gauge their chances of success. Apparently having decided that a chase was useless, they chose a faint easterly path into a sheltered valley of scrub trees. They soon left us far behind to explore new territory.

We followed a foot-wide game trail that branched off toward another more westerly area. It was used regularly, judging by the tufts of fur and dried scats that lay here and there. Burrows, once the home of small rodents, had been dug up and investigated. At one side, the bleached bones of an old wolf kill had been picked clean by ravens and other creatures. Charlie was fascinated by the smorgasbord of wild scents in the air. He continually sniffed the breeze for more. We entered a grove of twenty-foot-high trees at least three hundred years old. They were like bonsai, twisted from winter ice storms.

We stepped across a narrow stream, pausing to listen to the never-ending whisper of water, then trekked around a miniature lake, where a bull moose browsed alone on tender aquatic plants. Charlie jumped ahead to the end of his leash, wanting to give chase, but after a few tugs from Bill reluctantly gave up. Ahead lay a steep ridge.

As we carefully picked our way up the unstable rocks to the top, a howl seemed to come from the crest above us, followed by calls more distant. "There must be a strange pack somewhere to the west," Bill said.

Charlie's body was tense and alert. I instantly pulled him close for security, just in case we were about to encounter strange wolves who might regard him as a threat. It was more likely that they would run from us, I reassured myself.

With the last precarious footholds behind us, we reached the summit. As our breathing settled after the climb, we gasped in surprise. Our wolves had quickly circled through the rough terrain and were standing as still as statues two hundred feet ahead, staring at six wolves on the next ridge to the west.

Upon our arrival, the strangers spun in alarm to watch us, then nervously turned to depart. Alpha's howl stopped them in their tracks. Bill and I instantly stepped a few paces back and sat down with our eyes averted to indicate submission, while Charlie stood at our side, neither submissive nor assertive.

Still suspicious, the distant wolves stared for a minute or two. A thick-chested, almost completely black wolf with gray flecks, his authority evident in his firm stance, replied to Alpha's howl with a half-dozen warning barks. Alpha, his proud carriage projecting leadership, sent back a long, full-throated howl, while Mother, Denali, and Omega joined in different pitches.

As the howls slid down the scale to yips, the six strangers relaxed a little, still keeping an eye on us. They replied with shorter, higher calls. The echoes subsided into a silence that seemed to have a life of its own. No animosity appeared to exist between the two packs, only the friendly recognition of neighbors. The strangers appeared to be ignoring us, but Bill and I cautiously remained sitting.

Charlie now sat on his haunches alongside us, placidly watching the neighbors. He seemed to understand the situation, while we could only hope we were doing the right thing by demonstrating submission.

The abundant wolf scats and deep scratch marks on the ridge top were signs that wolves often frequented the area. Alpha scent-marked the spot, while his three companions watched the handsome gray-black stranger mark his pack's scent line. Then the two groups observed each other from their respective vantage points. Occasionally a wolf rose to urinate on or sniff scent marks, and sometimes even defecated, but each pack respected the other's territory.

Charlie continued to sit quietly, making no attempt to scent-mark. Bill and I sat still and avoided direct eye contact with the strangers. After a half hour, as if responding to a signal, the wolves of both sides rose to their feet and let loose with a long, jubilant howling that lasted for several minutes. Their spine-tingling song filled the valley, echoed off the mountainsides, then faded into the rustling of the chilling breeze.

With the concert finished, both families sniffed their own scent marks, then left in opposite directions. The strangers disappeared into the shadows of a deep ravine. Throughout the entire episode, none of the wolves attempted to cross the sedge- and lichen-covered area between the ridges. Scent marks were the "keep out" signs marking an area off limits by mutual agreement.

We couldn't discern whether the wolves had encountered each other purely by chance this time, but we suspected, judging by the scats and scratches on the ridge, that it was not their first meeting. The friendly atmosphere indicated that some of the wolves in each pack might even be related to each other. Wolf biologist David Mech, founder of the International Wolf Center in Ely, Minnesota, has found that wolves recognize relatives even after several years of separation. A noted expert on wolves, Mech has studied the animals in North America and the Arctic for more than thirty years. Young wolves sometimes leave the pack, or "disperse," according to Mech, to form their own family or join another pack. Some dispersal, which mixes genes with other families, is essential for the genetic health of the wolf population as a whole. If wolves remained for life with their birth family, inbreeding would eventually degrade the population's health with deformities and a decreased immune system.

Soon Charlie, Bill, and I were the only ones left on the ridge. We had set out to follow a hunting party and ended up watching our wolves pay a social call on the neighbors. Charlie adapted well and had not attempted any interaction, seeming to understand that his role was that of a visitor, not a participant.

We returned to camp following the wolves' shortcut. Now and then we caught a glimpse of the foursome trotting home through the trees, and we saw them again in the distance as they crossed the tundra.

Two hours later we arrived at camp, exhilarated by the day's unexpected events, only to be met by utter calm. One or two wolves looked up briefly from their naps as we approached. The pups were growling over a stick they coveted and didn't notice our arrival. While the wolves clearly took the day in stride, after dinner I spent two hours writing journal notes describing the events we had witnessed.

Once more we had observed wolves in a situation that humans rarely see. The friendly, unhurried atmosphere and the calm interaction between the two families were so different from the savage behavior often reported by those who hate wolves. Surely even those who wanted to destroy every last wolf, I thought, would change their minds had they been with us today. It was a privilege to observe such an intelligent, elegant species, and humbling to realize how our own human species often falls far short in comparison.

Attack

At 6 A.M. ONE MID-AUGUST morning, we hiked northwest in the silence of dense fog that filled the valley from floor to ridge top. We were following Alpha, Yukon, and Klondike, who were scent-marking. For twenty minutes, Alpha's black form led us through the mist. His blond companions were almost invisible. We soon lost sight of them all.

"Let's parallel this ridge," I said. "The fog could lift, and we might pick them up later."

"Okay, but I can hardly see five feet ahead," Bill said, nimbly sidestepping a tussock mound. "Hope we don't fall into a beaver pond."

When we stopped to take a compass bearing, a momentary lifting of the fog revealed three wolves—one dark mottled gray and two smaller blonds heavily streaked with gray—all of them different in coloring than any other wolf we had encountered. They were walking in single file along the crest above.

The fog closed. Hoping to see them again, we climbed through the dense mist to the fog-free summit, but they had disappeared, although all around lay dozens of bleached scats advertising a pack's frequent presence. The rocks had clearly been scent-marked and now smelled heavily of urine. We had stumbled onto a boundary area four miles northwest of our camp.

We immediately headed south, in the opposite direction from where we had seen the friendly neighboring pack a few days before, and continued deeper into the strangers' territory. I suddenly worried that an unfriendly new pack might object to Charlie, but Bill said if we kept him close he would be safe.

We crossed the gravel to begin our descent, but Charlie abruptly pulled back on his leash and steadfastly refused to continue. Puzzled, we all stopped. He tugged to go back in the direction we had come. Then it dawned on us. Charlie, who understood wolf boundaries better than we ever could, was refusing to enter deeper into another pack's territory. Feeling somewhat sheepish, we allowed him to lead us down the slope we had just climbed. Once on our pack's home ground, he relaxed.

"We should do what we first planned," I said as I tried to peer through the oppressive fog. "Parallel the ridge and hope this fog leaves soon."

Bill agreed as he checked the compass he kept on a leather strap around his neck. I kept mine in a handy top chest pocket to avoid the annoying pull on my neck, along with the GPS unit we used to check our position via satellite. A nearby splash warned us to swing south, where we followed a twisting route through a labyrinth of fog-shrouded beaver ponds.

An hour later, visibility improved. Mountaintops and ridges were in sharp relief in the sun's oblique rays. We again glimpsed the three strangers on a faint path a quarter mile away. Suddenly they split up: Two headed east, while the third swung west. In minutes, all three converged to take an easy route through our pack's valley. Charlie watched with only fleeting interest. We looked for signs of Alpha and the teens, but assumed they were too far away for us to see them.

Charlie stopped now and then to gaze into the lower valley. "Let's drop down," I said. "Charlie seems to think our pack is down there." I still felt uneasy about his safety, so close to strange wolves' territory, but Bill remained unconcerned.

Another hour later, as we were hiking around the marshy edges of a beaver pond, leaves suddenly crunched in the nearby trees. We froze. Three wolves—the same strangers we had seen earlier—confronted us.

The blond-gray pair kept their distance. The darker wolf, his fur ruff bristling, took three aggressive paces forward, his furious green eyes riveted on Charlie. Growls from deep within the wolf's throat rose to a vicious snarl. An unyielding Charlie stepped forward. Snarls vibrated his body as well. Bill and I both grabbed his leash, but he refused to retreat. Yelling the wildest sounds we could produce, we frantically threw chunks of dirt at the strangers.

But we were invisible in the angry standoff between the wolf and Charlie. He barked: one piercing, high-pitched bark followed by two more in quick succession. In seconds a black streak and two blond flashes erupted from the trees. Alpha, followed by the teens, was racing to take up the attack. Alpha's teeth flashed in a snarl as he stood between us and the other wolves. He steadily advanced on the dark one, who at this

The wolves live in the region of the Porcupine
caribou herd's wintering area.

unexpected confrontation retreated until he reached his two companions. As Alpha rushed at them, the three turned tail, raced up the nearby ridge, and disappeared over the crest into their own territory. Alpha and the teens dashed after them and were soon out of sight.

Relief engulfed us as our pounding hearts slowed. Our wolf friends had averted a crisis and possibly saved Charlie's life. Charlie acted as if nothing out of the ordinary had happened. He dug at a nearby lemming burrow and then, finding no one at home, rolled on the tiny hole. We, on the other hand, needed to pause and soothe our shattered nerves. We sat on the soft moss and leaned back against a convenient tree. Bill took out a thermos of hot chocolate. "Now I wish I'd paid more attention to your worrying over Charlie's safety," he said. "If we'd been alone, I'm sure those wolves would have run from us, but I misjudged what their reaction to Charlie would be."

After many years as equal partners in expeditions, having faced danger together so many times, we could often read each other's minds. There had been emergencies in the polar regions when high winds and plunging subzero temperatures made it almost impossible to erect our lifesaving tent. Without a word we always went into instant action, each attending to our own job, knowing just what we had to do because we'd practiced it together so many times.

I wondered whether the strange wolves had seen Charlie as a wolf rather than a dog, as a competitor they needed to eliminate. His defiant stance had delivered a challenge that no respectable wolf could ignore. When Charlie barked, he must have known all along that Alpha was fairly close and could help. Alpha's speed in response had been remarkable. His desire to protect his family's territory, and especially his defense of Charlie, made us feel even closer to this wild pack.

After a half-hour rest, we decided that we had had enough excitement for one day and headed back to camp, stopping only to replenish our supply of Labrador tea, cotton grass roots, and lichen. Alpha, Yukon, and Klondike did not return until dusk, when Charlie was already fast asleep on my sleeping bag.

Ten days later, just as a sea of fog rolled across the tundra and into our valley, we followed Alpha and the teens on a boundary scent-marking excursion. The three wolves loped slowly toward the ridge where we had recently seen the three aggressive strangers.

The wolves stopped frequently to scent-mark until they reached the summit which was clear of fog. They all stopped to urinate on several rocks. Alpha rubbed his neck on a stump then scratched dirt, each leg working as a stiff one-legged piston. Yukon defecated and, after a lengthy sniff of a gnarled log, marked it. After leaving ample warning to intruders, they all headed down a faint trail into the fog, then reappeared on the next ridge and repeated their routine. We kept pace with them as they methodically scent-marked the crest of several ridges, disposing of a few lemmings along the way. As evening approached, the fog lifted.

On one ridge Alpha sniffed a rock and then all three milled about, touching muzzles and wagging tails for several minutes before they calmed down and continued. Perhaps the scent contained a message from a strange wolf who had recently left his mark. After three miles, the threesome outdistanced us and disappeared into a valley. Leaving the wolves to continue marking their range, we returned to camp.

Numerous studies have been conducted concerning the size of wolf ranges. The general consensus is that they vary in size according to availability of prey and pack size. We were sure that the nearby ridge represented the southern boundary of this pack's hunting range. Their den and rendezvous sites were presumably located there because of the extreme security the area provided. Most of the family's range appeared to cover tundra with tree-covered valleys to the north and west.

As the August days slipped by, autumn crept in quietly. Tundra colors deepened and temperatures dropped to linger a few degrees below freezing. Four months after we had first arrived at Wolf Camp One, we awoke as storm clouds piled up from the north to herald the season's first snowstorm. By noon, the mountains lay behind a wall of thick gray clouds. All was hushed as the first flakes landed gently on the ground. Trees and willows were quietly cloaked in white, their branches bent under their autumn mantle.

All the wolves except Beta and the pups had already left before daylight to hunt. The pups quickly discovered a new game as they attempted to catch the flakes. Soon covered in white, they shook from end to end, showering nearby Beta, then joined him to lie under an overhanging rock, where they could wait for the hunters to return with breakfast.

After an hour, the sun emerged. The two inches of snow quickly turned to slush, and by midafternoon it had mostly disappeared. Temperatures rose to the low 40s for the next week in an unseasonably warm spell.

By now the pups had grown to resemble adults. Their soft, dark gray fur gradually turned blond like their mother's. Their bodies filled out, their legs were stronger, and their eyes, which had long ago lost their blueness, were changing to a yellow-green.

Beta took them on increasingly long walks. One day a pup proudly strode home with a lemming tightly grasped in his jaws. His brother promptly jumped him, trying to steal it. They squabbled over the dead body until Alpha pinned one pup to the ground and growled at the other. Then he stepped back, picked up the mangled lemming, chewed a moment, and swallowed as if to say, "If you're going to fight, then neither of you shall have it."

Bones in various stages of chewed destruction lay around the wolves' living area. After returning with Beta from forays to nearby ridges, the pups spent a substantial amount of time chewing these leftovers, while others became toys. One day, with Charlie looking on intently, a pup carefully dug a shallow hole behind one of Charlie's scent-marked rocks and buried a large moose leg bone there. After the pup left to join his brother and Yukon in a game of chase, Charlie dug up the bone and carried it to the side of the tent, where he promptly lay down and chewed it. Ownership had changed.

Yukon and Klondike, now disciplined members of the pack, hunted as frequently as the adults. Their howls had lost the reedy sound of the very young and taken on a deep, mature timbre. Sometimes they even returned carrying the largest portion of the prey, perhaps a lesson in building strength and stamina. But in spite of their growing stature within the pack, they still had pup-sitting duties when Beta and Mother rested.

One day a small rodent ran from behind our tent and across the den entrance. The pups gave chase at once. The game ended in disaster, as one pup miscalculated a sharp turn to cut off the rodent and crashed into his brother, sending him rolling. The crashee jumped to his feet and attacked the crasher in a fit of rage. Mother instantly grabbed the crashee's fur ruff and flipped him onto his back as he whimpered his apology. After she allowed him to get to his feet, he solemnly lay down to chew a bone as if nothing had happened. His brother gnawed another bone beside him.

Beta still hunted and appeared healthy and vigorous, but as summer became autumn, he looked older and moved more slowly. While Mother and the teenagers hunted frequently, more and more often Beta, the perfect guardian, stayed with the pups.

After the airplane incident, we concluded that this wolf pack had learned to watch the sky and listen for human hunters, and then taught their offspring to do the same. Our theory was reinforced as we noticed the pups being taught this behavior. One afternoon in near-freezing temperatures, made colder by the light northerly wind, we heard the faint sound of a distant plane flying low across the tundra. All of us—wolves and humans—were instantly alert.

As the sound drifted away, we beheld the comical sight of Beta, up on the ridge, instructing the pups in how to watch for planes. First he cocked his head toward the heavens for a moment, then looked down at the two pups. When he received no reaction, he patiently repeated the process. Although the brothers gave Beta their full attention, they were clearly puzzled.

Giving up for the moment, Beta lay down. The two young wolves were on him in an instant, tugging his fur and attacking his tail. Then they changed tactics and stepped back a few feet. Both crouched in their best hunting style and slowly crept up on Beta, cautiously placing each front paw in front of the other. In unison, they leaped at his throat and shoulder, attacking as never before, growling and tugging. Although superb hunting practice, it was more than Beta could tolerate. He heaved himself to his feet, shedding his tormentors.

After a vigorous shake, he resumed the sky-watching lesson. This time his patience had its reward: The pups caught on and glanced up with him. The next day Beta again took both students to the ridge top for more practice. From then on, they sometimes looked up, without adult urging, when a plane was heard. The human quality of this behavior—the ability to teach offspring survival tactics—made it the most fascinating one we observed, and proof of the wolves' profound intelligence.

Under a night lit by a full moon, we happened to awake just as a group prepared to leave on a hunt. Denali ran down from his watch post to greet Alpha, who lifted his nose, pursed his lips, and sent a long low wail through the valley, across the tree-tops, all the way to the tundra. Others joined in, and soon even the pups' reedy voices joined the songfest. The family's music rang out, mingling with the soft moonlight.

Finally, when the sound had died away on the gentle breeze, all the adults filed into the forest. The evening hunt had begun. This was the first time the family had left the pups entirely alone.

Four hours later, just before dawn broke across the ridges, distant howls signaled the hunters' return. Arriving with the back leg of a sheep and two hares, they lay everything on the ground for the pups, who tore into the offerings. As was often the case, the hunters' distended bellies showed that they had eaten their fill at the kill site.

Wolves are remarkable eating machines. They gobble their food at tremendous speed and crack even large moose bones easily. Biologist David Mech has calculated that an adult's stomach can hold as much as twenty pounds of meat at one time. When prey is available, wolves gorge themselves and then sleep.

Although wolves eat formidable amounts when they find prey, they can endure long periods of fasting. In some places such as the polar Arctic, distances are vast and food is scarce. Hunts sometimes take wolves twenty or more miles from a den.

It is important for wolves to hunt successfully during the summer months to ensure that they enter winter in good condition. Judging by how much food these wolves carried to the den and rendezvous site, they ate well. They appeared healthy and content. Because they lived in an area of abundant prey, they seldom traveled far and never went more than two days between hunts all summer long.

Soon after dawn the sun climbed over the mountains to turn the frost crystals into millions of sparkling diamonds. Bill, Charlie, and I set out to explore a low ridge a mile from our camp. The low tundra plants had reached their full autumn splendor of fiery red, and the deciduous willows blazed yellow and orange. A faint game path led upward, then faded as we left the valley and began a gradual climb through scree and scattered trees.

We had just paused to drink from our water bottles when Charlie whimpered and turned to face the direction we had come. To our surprise, Beta and the two pups were following us. When we stopped, they sat and waited until we hiked ahead. We trekked across the slope with the three shadowing us. Although we slowed often to see if Beta wanted to catch up, he traveled no closer. Similarly, Charlie showed no desire to join Beta and the pups, calmly striding ahead of Bill and me with hardly a backward glance. We scaled a gentle slope to a low ridge and sat on a boulder. Charlie still showed no interest in our companions.

While we rested, the pups explored and dug for lemmings, which lived in the burrows between the rocks. The sight was hilarious. The pups scratched at such a furious pace that dirt flew in all directions. Thrusting their heads into each hole, they twice emerged with a tiny, squirming bundle that they quickly dispatched with a crunch and a gulp. Obsessed with the burrows, they seemed unlikely to be attracted by the smell of our food, but we kept our munchies in our packs anyway, agreeing that it was better to take no chances.

After an hour's entertainment, we returned to camp with Charlie in the lead. Beta and the pups remained on the ridge, and later accompanied us at a distance, just as any group of friends might enjoy a stroll in the wilderness. Now and then the youngsters leaped at something on one side of the trail, and Beta stopped to scent-mark twice. Once he rolled and squirmed on something on the ground, all four feet in the air. The pups copied him, more clumsily, in the same spot.

Back at camp the rest of the wolves were spread out, still sleeping off their early-morning meal. As we passed, Alpha raised his head, yawned hugely, and went back to sleep. Instead of stopping at the rendezvous site, Beta and the pups continued behind us for the short distance to our camp. The threesome inspected the old den site for a few minutes before returning to their area, where they lay down for a nap in the shade of boulders. Charlie lay in the shade of the tent. The walk was over, and all had earned a rest.

One cool afternoon at the end of August, while all the wolves except Mother and Beta were out hunting, the thirteen-week-old pups were moved to a second rendezvous site only two hundred yards from the first. Mother set out with the brothers frolicking close behind, while Beta brought up the rear. The spot was a shallow dugout, sheltered by dwarf spruces and rock buttresses, with a beaver pond a quarter mile away. This flat area provided more space for the fast-growing pups. When the hunters returned, they dropped a meal of a partially consumed Dall sheep at the new site. The pups, Mother, and Beta ate their fill.

By the time the family established the second rendezvous site, we were even more convinced that the family was unwilling to leave the area's safety to establish rendezvous sites farther away. The pups weren't yet ready to move long distances with the pack. Perhaps the episode with the aerial hunters had caused the wolves to seek increased security, even if it meant delaying movement of the pups.

With winter just around the corner it was time to decide when we would leave the area and begin our preparation for the second phase of our adventure, our winter expedition to northern Canada. After our departure, this pack would begin their winter travels throughout their hunting range as soon as the pups were ready for extended travel.

We knew we wanted to stay into the first weeks of October, which necessitated a re-supply. To avoid subjecting Charlie to another unhappy parting from his wolf friends. Bill volunteered to hike out alone and return with food and fuel. Charlie and I would remain behind, an arrangement that would also prevent the possible destruction of our gear by curious wolves.

Although temperatures were already hovering around freezing, Bill left his sleeping bag and the spare tent behind to allow more room in his pack for supplies. After calling Margaret on

*When a game becomes too serious, a showing of long white
fangs warns off the offender.*

the radio, he packed and headed down the valley. Charlie followed him as far as his lead would allow, watching and barking
until Bill disappeared. At the sound of Charlie's barks Alpha,
Denali, and Omega came running and silently watched Bill
walk away. Then they set out to follow, returning four hours
later.

Later Bill told me he was surprised to find himself accompanied by the three wolves for the first few miles. After a two-day
hike he met Margaret, loaded his pack with all he could carry
and headed back. At night he snuggled into his bivvy sack wear-
ing all his clothes to keep barely warm.

Charlie and I spent the next five days hiking to the ridge
tops. On the fifth evening Charlie signaled Bill's return by
bounding about and barking excitedly. After helping Bill unload
his heavy pack I cooked dinner, and as we ate Charlie sat at

Bill's side. That night he slept across Bill's sleeping bag. Clearly he was glad to have Bill back in camp.

One early September morning we hiked out of camp as shafts of light filtered through the mountains. The wolves had already left for a hunt. We climbed to our lookout spot above the junction and scanned the tundra, but saw no sign of the wolves.

The early brilliance highlighted the red and gold carpet of low plants that persisted through the shallow snow. In the spare, wide-open space, plant life is so fragile and the air is so incredibly fresh. "This is what makes me come alive," I said, taking a deep breath of the crisp air. "I could live here forever."

Bill said it was the tundra that fascinated him. "So many times I've flown over tundra without really appreciating it," he said. "When I look at the plants and realize what they have put up with to grow at all, it makes everything else seem unimportant. We're looking at vegetation that's taken hundreds of years to grow inches."

We sat for an hour, saying little, enjoying the quiet beauty that settled over us as gently as a feather. By now we both knew it was going to be harder for us to leave than we had ever imagined.

Later, some distance away, an antlered caribou trotted from the trees onto the tundra, soon followed by a dozen more. Through binoculars we sighted seven wolves, led by Denali, bursting from the forest and charging after the caribou, who took instant flight.

Then two dropped back. The wolves split up and chased both. One whirled to face its pursuers. Three wolves closed in, careful to stay out of range of hooves and antlers. As the caribou spun again, a wolf leaped at its flank, slashed its hide, and jumped away. Bleeding heavily, the beast lunged. The three wolves charged, knocking the caribou to the ground. It kicked for only seconds. The hunters tore through the thick hide. The other four wolves had already pulled their quarry down and ripped open its belly.

Seconds later, fifteen caribou breached the trees, saw the wolves, and bounded away in long strides across the tundra. As the feast continued, a dark figure emerged from the woods.

A grizzly bear walked toward the wolves, his nose raised, having caught the caribou scent. Twenty yards from the carcass, the bear paused. With a snarl, Alpha lunged at him. The bear hurriedly backed away a few paces and sat down. Alpha returned to his meal but looked up now and then to check the bear, who remained motionless. Minutes later, the three wolves nearest the grizzly left their carcass to join the others at the second kill close by. The grizzly walked to the first, then set about gnawing and tearing at the partly consumed body. Four cawing ravens, who had been circling in wide loops above the kill, landed to share the meal. The bear showed no visible reaction to the ravens, who pecked greedily at the far edge of the carcass. As the wolves tore into the second animal, they seemed oblivious to their feasting neighbors. In twenty minutes the pack had eaten their fill and sat cleaning themselves, while the bear and the ravens continued to eat.

After the wolves had licked themselves clean and rolled in the coarse sedges, they rose as a group. With raised hackles, they charged the bear and ravens. The bear ambled to a low rise a short distance away, while the ravens, with loud squawks of protest, swirled overhead. After ripping chunks of meat off the carcass, the wolves headed home, each with as much as they could carry. The bear and the ravens now had the leftovers to themselves.

As the food disappeared, though, it was the bear's turn to chase the ravens away. They hopped barely out of range of the bear's snapping jaws. The last scraps were the bear's to keep.

Two formidable hunting species, wolves and bears are normally considered enemies, but here they had agreed to share food. Even the ravens were welcomed. The wolves appeared to readily tolerate the bear's presence, on their terms. Perhaps the wolves, who had the upper hand in the encounter, had sensed that there was plenty for all. The episode contrasted dramatically with the pack's behavior in an earlier grizzly encounter, when they had fiercely defended their pups from a bear approaching the den. The difference? In that case their young's lives were in danger from an adversary capable of killing and eating them.

I wondered how prevalent such sharing was. It is generally believed that animals defend their kills from other species and even from each other, and that sharing is not a survival skill in the wild. But we had seen something different.

Throughout North America, wolves and bears share the same territory. Bears have been known to kill pups, but usually only when a bear stumbled onto a den defended by a single wolf. Although bears' sharp claws, powerful shoulders, and massive teeth that can crush a skull are formidable weapons, and evidence of bears killing adult wolves does exist, biologist David Mech has found that the species usually avoid each other.

As we returned to camp, Bill wondered aloud. "Is it possible that some species instinctively understand, at a primitive level, that they're just a single link in the environmental chain—that to survive, everyone must survive?" We hoped to explore such questions further in the winter, when we would travel farther north to encounter arctic foxes and polar bears as well as wolves.

Close to camp, we startled a group of caribou grazing on spruce boughs. In an instant they raced away, almost without a sound. Because the wolf family's territory was situated in the northern region of the Porcupine caribou herd's wintering grounds, the supply of prey would remain adequate throughout the winter. For thousands of years the herd of about 240,000 has continued a pattern of migration four hundred miles north across the Porcupine River to the coastal plain of Alaska's Arctic National Wildlife Reserve, where their calves are born. In August, with new calves at their side, they migrate back to overwinter in their traditional grounds.

The annual migration is the basis of sustenance for the Gwich'in people, a native culture of about 7,000 who live along the migratory route. Calling themselves "the people of the caribou," the Gwich'in have a lifestyle that is traditionally interwoven with that of the Porcupine caribou herd.

🐾

My journal writing prompted some interesting interactions with the wolves. One day a loose page from my journal fluttered on the breeze to land ten feet over the wolves' boundary line. The page contained my notes carefully describing a howling session.

Without thinking, I crossed the invisible scent boundary and bent to pick up the page, but looked up just as my hand reached the paper. Alpha had silently approached and stood three feet away. He glanced at the page for a moment and then, with his head cocked to one side, his yellow eyes met mine with a soft but inquiring expression.

I straightened slowly and stepped back. Alpha came forward, took the page in his mouth, and turned toward the rendezvous site. I hoped I could get him to drop the notes. They represented many hours of work, and I wasn't about to give them up without protest. I forced myself to extend my hand. "Alpha, that page is mine," I said softly.

At the sound of my voice, he stopped and looked back. His steady eyes gave me a look of understanding. Keeping my hand extended, I continued to speak to him in quiet, even tones. With his gaze still fixed on mine, he dropped the paper and then strolled to a shady rock with a barely perceptible fanning of his tail.

I retrieved the page, hoping I appeared more at ease than I felt as I walked back to the tent. Bill returned from washing a shirt in the stream, having watched the entire episode. We agreed that it was another signal of acceptance. Alpha could easily have kept my precious notes, or even urinated on them in a display of dominance, but he chose to treat me as a friend instead.

During an eight-day spell of unusually mild weather, the mosquito swarms that had survived the early August frost blossomed again. Seeking to escape them, we decided to flee to the windy ridges. Bill and Charlie climbed eastward to explore, while I chose a spot closer to camp to catch up on my journal. I sat on a just-right rock, one with a backrest conveniently carved by nature.

Shortly my attention turned to Denali, who was hurrying up the trail toward me to seek refuge from the mosquitoes. The trail passed within two feet of me. I bent over my notes, pretending not to notice him. He hustled by without so much as a pause or a sideways look, ignoring my existence entirely. He had places

Denali endures mosquitoes by the stream. Breezy ridgetops are the wolves' only escape.

to go, and this human he had studied for so long didn't warrant his attention anymore.

I expected him to continue on to a place of his own choosing. Instead, with his back to me, he sat down directly behind me on the path, twenty feet away. We were two friends sharing the same desire to escape the whining pests. Later Omega passed by, also without visible reaction. Some sign of recognition would have been nice, I thought, but then again, I had been paid a compliment. I was so trusted there was no need to keep an eye on me.

I wrote in my journal, describing this new and surprising event, for another hour. Before returning to camp, I tossed a small rock a few feet along the ridge to see if I could gain the wolves' attention. Denali opened a sleepy eye but, seeing that it was only me, went back to sleep.

That night I read my journal notes to Bill. The last entry read, "Today these wolves taught me the real meaning of unconditional trust. To be so trusted is an experience I shall never forget."

Parting

A HARD SEPTEMBER WIND swept through the mountains from the north to signal the first blast of winter. Heavier frosts blanketed the tundra, and a skim of ice covered the ponds, while the shallow pools were frozen solid. Temperatures dropped into the 20s. Snow showers blanketed Wolf Camp One every few days, covering the mountains in a white mantle. Yellow willow leaves drifted to earth, and fiery red tundra plants disappeared beneath the snow. The shimmering greens, pinks, and blues of the aurora borealis, or northern lights, were visible in the lengthening darkness. An Arctic winter's deep cold had begun its slow spread across the land.

Although the pups now traveled longer distances, they still had not joined the pack in a hunt of large animals. They caught lemmings and other rodents close to home and now and then returned with a hare.

One mid-September morning, more than five months after we first arrived at Wolf Camp One, we explored an area three miles away. We crossed ridges dusted with snow and traversed valleys where drifts had accumulated in pockets of willow thickets. Inches-deep surface water lay frozen in the 24-degree air.

After a two-hour trek, we climbed to the top of a ridge and walked along its crest above a deserted beaver swamp. A quarter mile beyond we saw a picturesque lake, rich in aquatic plants, no more than two feet deep and two hundred feet wide, nestled in the tundra at the edge of a taiga forest. Animal tracks in the scant snow cover radiated from the water's edge.

At my approach the mother raises her head with a loud snort, warning me that my unexpected interruption to their foraging is unwelcome.

As we approached the lake, a startled lynx scurried to the protection of willows and spruce.

At the sight of two hares hopping past the far shore, Charlie tried to give chase. We pulled him back. Disgruntled, he barked in protest. The shadowy form of a female moose, barely visible through the branches on the far side of the lake, quickly withdrew into the dense undergrowth.

"A perfect place to live," I said, soaking up the tranquil scene.

"But a bit far to walk out for groceries," Bill quipped.

We followed a trail to the far side. At an abrupt turn, we saw a flicker of motion as another lynx silently retreated into the brush.

After a lunch break under a weak sun, we headed back to camp. Storm clouds had built on the horizon. Just as we crossed the ridge, I remembered a lens cap I had left at our picnic spot. Bill agreed to wait with Charlie while I went back.

At the lake I was surprised to encounter a hulking mother moose and her calf grazing on the near side, pulling up chunks of aquatic plants. At my approach, the mother moose raised her head with a loud snort, warning me that my unexpected interruption to their foraging was unwelcome. Both animals' highly sensitive ears pointed in my direction, tuned to the slightest sound. Their dark eyes watched me intently.

Concerned that the mother might charge in defense of her calf, I waited, motionless. After a long minute of appraisal, mother and calf finally relaxed. The mother bent to pull another mouthful of grass. The calf reached beneath her belly to suckle.

Congratulating myself for stumbling across such an excellent photo opportunity, I slowly reached for my camera and became engrossed in finding just the right angle. After shooting two frames, I bent to change the film. I didn't notice that the female had once more turned toward me. Only when she picked up speed and splashed through the shallows in my direction did I realize the danger.

Terrified, still clutching my camera, I raced back the way I had come, finding speed I didn't know I was capable of. But I was no match for her anger and long legs. As I frantically reached for every bit of acceleration I could muster, she quickly caught up and, with a tremendous, bone-shaking thump, smashed me to the ground with her thick-boned forehead.

Immediately I covered my head, expecting her to strike with her lethal front hooves, but my racing heart and mind met only silence. I dared not move and prayed as never before.

After several minutes that seemed like hours, the moose turned and splashed into the lake. I looked carefully over my shoulder in time to see her rejoin her calf. I shakily rose to my feet as the two evaporated into the surrounding brush and trees.

Now the only sign of the entire incident was a few ripples on the water.

Still shaking, but relieved to have suffered only bruises, I returned to Charlie and Bill, who was unsympathetic. "That was a stupid thing to do," he said succinctly.

He was right. Moose cows with calves are notoriously cantankerous and aggressive. I would never forget this lesson.

We arrived in camp just as a frigid wind picked up and the first snowflakes fell. The fast-moving storm passed in an hour, leaving our site bathed in sunlight. But the light contained little heat and couldn't melt the inch of new snow.

Due to the increased hours of darkness, nighttime observation of hunts was now impossible. Just before daylight in the second week of September, we hiked to our lookout above the junction in hopes of watching the pack leave to hunt. The entire family, except the pups and Beta, trotted our way. They paused to scent-mark the rock and the old snag at the junction, then paralleled our ridge before cutting through a low pass to a valley just beyond.

We quickly trekked along and took a shortcut to a high knoll. Below us, the wolves stopped just as they reached the edge of the scrub trees. Prey was just ahead, judging by their excited milling about and tail wagging. In moments they fanned out. Denali and Omega swept to the left, racing ahead through the cover of the surrounding brush, while Alpha, Yukon, and Klondike stayed back. Suddenly Denali and Omega cut right and chased four Dall sheep out of the undergrowth, back across a clearing, and toward the three crouching wolves, who remained concealed on the edge of thick vegetation beneath spruce trees.

Just as the first sheep raced by, all three wolves leaped at it. Alpha grabbed the sheep's nose, while Yukon and Klondike tackled the flanks. The sheep, with a terrified scream, collapsed beneath the weight of a flurry of wolves, who raked its body with their teeth. After a last few convulsions, all life was gone. The other three sheep veered sharply away as their leader fell.

The pack set to work to eat its fill. In twenty minutes the sheep was reduced to a skeleton. The wolves chewed bones for the next hour, then set off again in search of more prey.

They traveled through a narrow ravine a hundred yards ahead of and below us. After noting the direction they were headed, we took a shorter route, then descended to cross a meadow. We climbed another minor ridge, arriving at the crest in time to see the wolves stalking three sheep, this time all rams, using similar tactics as before.

Denali raced ahead and angled across to cut the sheep off from the open tundra. The confused sheep turned abruptly as one to flee down a shallow gully. The waiting wolves, led by Omega, ran across the lower gully with bodies slung low to a hiding place on the edge of sparsely growing willows to intersect the fleeing sheep.

Just as the sheep came abreast of the ambushing wolves, Omega leaped out to grab the throat of the first, while Denali caught the second sheep by its flank just as Alpha sprang and clung to its nose, dragging it down. Meanwhile, Omega, hanging on with all his strength, was dragged through the wil-

A startled lynx scurries to the protection of willows.

lows by the first big, powerful ram. Klondike leaped onto the sheep's back and sank her teeth into a shoulder as Yukon grabbed a rear leg. The ram kicked violently, sending Yukon tumbling to land several feet away. Instantly she was on her feet and leaping at the ram's neck.

With loud bleats of terror both sheep valiantly fought back but finally were no match for the attacking wolves. Minutes after the ambush began, both lay dead. As the wolves tore into the carcasses, the third ram raced to safety. After thirty minutes of gorging, the pack walked a few yards away to lick their paws and bodies clean, thus allowing the ravens, who had been circling overhead with raucous caws, to swoop down and eat. They chattered loudly with excitement as they swarmed the remains.

Wolves' sharp front teeth are well suited for slashing and clinging. Their imposing fangs, or canine teeth, combined with the powerful clamp of their incisors, enable wolves to grip and hang on to their victims, as we had just witnessed. Molars not only crush bones but tear off large chunks of meat, which wolves can then bolt down with little or no chewing. According to biologist David Mech, whole body parts and large chunks of unchewed meat have been found in wolves' stomachs.

An hour later the wolves repossessed both carcasses from the ravens and tore the remains to pieces. Then, with the ravens flying ahead to herald their triumph, each wolf set out for the trek back with a chunk of sheep held crosswise in powerful jaws. All that was left at the kill site was blood-soaked earth and snow and a few tufts of wool.

The two hunts had been a masterfully orchestrated group effort and were similar in method. Although Denali was the hunt leader, each wolf appeared to know his or her role. They had acted in unison, without waiting for a boss to issue instructions. Having cooperated many times, the pack knew each other's abilities. They sensed just the right moment to cut off a sheep in midflight or chase it back into an ambush. Clearly the wolves' traits of individual strength, lightning speed, and intelligence were the components of success.

The notion that wolves kill at will was disproved by their many unsuccessful hunting attempts. Most animals, especially those as large as or larger than a wolf, possess enough agility and speed to escape the jaws of hungry wolves. As a result it is the sick, old, and very young that usually fall to wolf predation. Moose are perhaps the wolf's most dangerous prey. According to Mech, a moose that steadfastly stands its ground is often left alone.

We returned to camp feeling subdued. We understood the laws of nature. One species must live off a weaker species. Nevertheless, we both admitted that in our hearts we had rooted for the sheep to escape. Whenever we watched a hunt it was always a heart-wrenching experience to see magnificent animals die so violently. However, our sadness was always tempered by the knowledge that death had come quickly and the family needed the food to survive. We had had the rare opportunity to witness, up close in one day, two successful hunts in the wild that ended with wolves sharing their life-giving food supply with the ravens. There is a gentleness in nature that offsets the violence of having to kill to survive.

Charlie remained quiet throughout the chase but growled with excitement, hackles raised, during the final kill. Halfway back to camp, as we trekked through a shallow valley, five sheep stopped on a trail two hundred feet above us, stared briefly, and then ran, their hooves a blur of speed. Charlie leaped to the end of his leash, jerking Bill off his feet. Charlie seemed not to notice as he pulled Bill forward. I sprang to grab the leash too, and with our combined effort we stopped Charlie, much to his dismay. After witnessing two hunts in one day, he was so excited that he was more than ready to conduct his own hunt. Not until we approached the outskirts of camp did he consent to walk forward instead of looking back in the direction of the sheep, who had long since disappeared.

We arrived in camp just as darkness approached. All was silent. The entire wolf family was sprawled about, sleeping off their meal. Even the ravens were quiet.

Charlie looks back. He doesn't want to leave.

Toward the end of September, we awoke to winter's first serious snowfall. In three hours, the snow was four inches thick. We needed to plan our departure before the onset of deep winter.

The snow accumulating on the ground over the next several weeks would provide insulation for those animals who hibernated during the winter, as well as for those large and small creatures who continued to hunt throughout the dark months. Animals sheltering in tunnels beneath a foot of snow would enjoy temperatures many degrees warmer than those above.

A blizzard heralded the first week of October. We had been living beside the den for almost six months. The well-fed pack was in good flesh, ready for the winter. With increasing frequency the pups traveled longer distances from the den under strict supervision, sometimes for most of the night and all day. Packs normally leave the last rendezvous site at the beginning of winter, so we knew the entire family would soon be departing to hunt and travel the full range of their territory.

The brothers, who now resembled adults, would go with the group. With their pups accompanying them, wolves can travel over a much wider hunting area in winter, since they do not have to return to den sites until spring. Then the group either goes to an old site, as this family had, or digs a new den in another area to accommodate the next litter of pups.

But Bill, Charlie, and I had to leave. Dreading the parting, we delayed it as long as possible, knowing it would be wrenching for us and even more so for Charlie. When we had first arrived at the den, we resolved not to become emotionally bonded to the pack, but it took only a short time for us to understand the special privilege they had given us.

We could not remain emotionally separate from these intelligent, wild hunters who at times acted like playful children. As we lived close to them and learned of the challenges they faced, we found ourselves caught up in their daily lives. We grew to love them and to appreciate how much they had to teach us. They had captured our hearts.

As for Charlie, he seemed thoroughly enthralled with the wolves and his life in the wild. We knew he wouldn't want to leave.

But we had come prepared only for summer and autumn. We knew that once the pack left to travel their winter range, we could never keep up with them. With just four days of food left, we had to depart before any more winter blizzards arrived.

With our two-way radio turned on, we waited for Margaret's transmission. At 10 A.M. the silence was broken by static and the faint sound of her voice. We fiddled with the dials until she came through more clearly, then made final arrangements to meet her at the Dempster Highway in three days.

At daybreak the next morning, we packed our gear. We folded our sadly abused tent, which the wolves had reduced to a barely functional model. The rest of our things had fared relatively well: a few teeth marks on various items, and some corners chewed off in odd places. We stowed everything in our rapidly expanding packs.

We bundled up the garbage, which was minimal because of our simple diet. We filled the deep latrine with soil, covering it with the original sod, which we had carefully kept alive at the side of the stream.

Charlie sat close to the den, watching us prepare to leave. Suddenly he gave the most mournful howl we had ever heard. The entire pack, even the pups, joined him at his boundary. They all sensed our imminent departure. Bill and I paused where our tent had stood and spoke to the wolves. We made no sense to them, of course, but we hoped we might communicate our love and respect.

We also promised them we would return. Weeks ago, we had decided that we must come back the next summer, and for several more, to make sure the wolves had remained safe from hunters. The only way we could leave them was to know we would see them again.

Finally it was time to leave. We both stood facing the family to bid our farewell, fighting tears as we looked across at the group. "If only we could know they'll come to no harm, it would be easier," I said. We had talked for many hours about how we could protect the family, but in the end we concluded that all we could do was keep the den's exact location a secret forever.

One by one I called to them by name and said good-bye.

Bill did the same. "We won't forget you," he said.

We lifted our packs and struggled into the shoulder straps, then sadly turned toward the valley. But Charlie refused to budge. He stood facing the wolves. We sat with him and cried.

While Bill held Charlie close, I explained to him, "Charlie, winter's here. We have to leave. We can't leave you behind."

He seemed to sense our emotions. He turned to leave, looked back at his friends for one or two minutes, and then licked my hand.

With the wolves watching, we left the meadow we had called home for almost six months, and the wild family we had become a part of. As we stepped across the stream, we saw Mother and the pups sitting dejectedly on our tent's spot. The teenagers, who had now grown into two elegant young adults, gathered near Mother and the pups. They all gave a mournful howl.

Alpha yipped twice. Then, accompanied by Denali, Beta, and Omega, he followed us for the next three hours. As we crossed a ridge, Charlie raised his muzzle to the sky for one last cry with his friends. They all howled together for ten minutes, a heart-rending sound. Then the wolves turned and slowly began to walk back in the direction of their den. Several times they stopped to look back as Charlie watched them leave. Finally they were gone. A subdued Charlie led us away. Bill and I followed in silence.

When at last we met Margaret, she immediately understood the difficulty of our departure. She hugged us and helped us load our gear onto the truck. Charlie received a large piece of his favorite beef jerky as a reward for his job well done.

Before we climbed in for the long drive home, Bill and I embraced. Our journey had been more successful than we could have ever imagined. We would return to visit our summer wolves. But in the meantime, our thoughts turned to our upcoming adventure among the winter wolves.

Winter

Arctic

WE SPENT NOVEMBER AND DECEMBER training in the untamed areas of the Cascade Range, skiing and pulling sleds. We experimented to find the fastest way to erect a tent in a storm and the best way to load a sled so it would pull evenly. We amassed winter food supplies and tapped the polar clothing and equipment stockpile in our basement. After years of expeditions to the remote corners of the world, we have a wide variety of gear suitable for any climate.

To add to our first six months' success, we sought to reach beyond the summer den and travel to the icy shores of northern Canada, where polar bears hunt seals on the sea ice. We would go all the way to the northern islands at the edge of the polar sea ice that marks the western beginning of the Northwest Passage, exploring the area for wolves and polar bears. On numerous occasions we had seen wolves traveling across the frozen ocean following the bears. The question we wanted to explore was why wolves travel onto the sea ice far from shore, where their normal land prey does not exist.

Just as we had seen wolves, ravens, and grizzly bears in the Yukon living in close proximity to each other and even sharing food, we hoped to encounter wolves, polar bears, and arctic foxes as we skied across the winter land and sea ice to learn more about the cohabitation of these fascinating animals in the harshest environment on Earth.

New maps, with a route drawn in that began at Inuvik, a remote Canadian Northwest Territories town, covered our kitchen table. The black line continued north, more than a hundred miles across the immense Mackenzie River Delta to Canada's austere northern coast and Tuktoyaktuk—known locally as "Tuk," meaning "resembling caribou" in Inuktitut, the Inuit language.

From there the line continued across the map at least fifty miles beyond the coast, over the frozen Beaufort Sea, which joins the ice of the Arctic Ocean. Our northernmost point would be tiny uninhabited Pullen Island, north of Richards Island, locked in the winter grip of the polar ice pack. From Pullen Island we would ski back to Tuk, then to a place in the interior of the Mackenzie Delta where our Inuk friend John had told us we would find a wolf family at their winter rendezvous. Our theory was that, by heading for Pullen Island, we would cover enough distance on the sea ice to maximize our chances of encountering wolves and polar bears.

Our winter journey would be quite different from our summer experience. We would be constantly moving through dangerous sea ice as we sought to discover more about the relationship between wolves and polar bears. As we searched out our wolf subjects on the frozen ocean, we would face the added challenge of traveling and camping close to polar bears, among the most dangerous of all carnivores.

John's discovery of a pack who gathered together between hunts on the delta would make it possible to camp close to landbound wolves for a lengthy period, rather than face the impossible task of following wolves on foot as they traveled throughout their winter hunting range.

John, whom we had met two years ago on a previous journey to his town, was a tall, slender, reclusive man (so much so that he insisted we not use his real name in this story). He had given up alcohol after his brother almost killed a man during a drunken brawl several years before. John had spent fifteen years living and working in the southern Yukon city of Whitehorse before leaving his job and moving to Cambridge Bay. Once an ardent wolf hunter, he had undergone a life-changing experience when he happened upon a thin, sad-eyed female wolf tied with a ten-foot chain to a fence in a backyard. He bought the animal for fifty dollars, named her Lucky, and turned her loose into the wild.

When he released her from a large dog-carrying crate she began to run, then stopped and looked back at him with upturned lips, as if smiling her thanks. As he watched her disappear, he vowed never to hunt wolves again. "I'll never forget her expression and the look in her eyes," he told us. "She trusted me. I'll never betray her trust as long as I live."

As part of our preparation, John phoned us with regular updates on weather and sea ice conditions. He also gave us the news we had hoped for: While seal hunting, he had sighted several wolves and polar bears on the frozen ocean along our proposed route. Also, he reported that the land-bound wolf family he had discovered, which had the unusual habit of returning

Our camp in a windstorm.

regularly throughout the winter to one place on the delta, was following their normal cycle.

Thoroughly prepared and brimming with enthusiasm, Bill, Charlie, and I set out the following January to drive by pickup truck to Dawson City. Our skis and sleds were tied down in the back, along with our packs and supplies. Charlie occupied the backseat—that is, until he decided he wanted a turn in the front seat. Whoever wasn't driving climbed out to exchange seats with Charlie until he later signaled with barks that he wanted his own seat back.

The countryside had changed since last summer's journey. The land hid beneath a snowy blanket. The rivers were frozen and snowmobiles were parked in front yards or dashing along trails. In Dawson City, snow was pushed into piles here and there. Gray slush replaced the puddles of last year.

After one night in Dawson City we found Ted, whom we had met the previous year, still working in the grocery store. A lanky, gray-haired fortysomething transplant from the lower forty-eight, he had been so fascinated by Charlie during our visit to Dawson last summer that he made us promise to look him up on our return so he could spend time with his "favorite dog." We took it as no insult that he had not mentioned wanting to meet Bill and me again. We were used to Charlie taking center stage.

Much to Ted's delight, we left Charlie in his charge while we searched for a newspaper to catch up on the local news. We bought some postcards and hastily scribbled a note on each, then returned to the store to find Ted in loud conversation with everyone within earshot about Charlie's many virtues. Charlie eagerly licked every hand that reached out to pat him. He was a big hit and he knew it. Finally we said good-bye, but only after we promised to return with Charlie after our winter journey was over.

We left town and took the frozen Dempster Highway across the Yukon Territory and the Northwest Territories border to Inuvik. Here we would begin the winter stage of our yearlong wolf project. The road, although slippery and treacherous in places, was less hazardous to tires now that the shale was covered with packed snow. Even so, we carried two spares in addition to five gallons of gas. Due to the reduced daylight, which consisted of only a few hours of gray light, we stopped halfway and camped at Eagle Plains.

The next day we set out at 7 A.M., before daylight, to complete our journey to Inuvik. Along the way we passed through the wintering grounds of the Porcupine caribou herd, an area where the animals paw beneath a thin covering of snow to find a meal of willows, sedges, and lichen.

We paused at the lonely roadside spot where Margaret had left us last spring for our hike to the wolf den. We reminisced about the summer as we looked toward the valleys and mountains we had traversed in last spring's thaw. Wispy clouds swept across the mountaintops. The slopes were shrouded in white, and the valleys lay frozen and still.

The den and rendezvous sites would be empty now. The family would be traveling with the pups throughout their hunting range. The pups would be big enough to keep up with the adults and learn to hunt large prey. The discipline taught by the family, particularly Beta, would help them become shrewd hunters.

We longed to see them again and know they were safe, but we would have to wait until next spring's denning season before we could visit. In the meantime, I took out a walnut-size brown rock I had collected from the den entrance. I had vowed to carry it with me during our winter journey and told Bill that it would bring us good luck in our quest to meet wolves on the sea ice and winter land. But my secret reason for carrying it was that this small rock was a link to the family we loved. I held it to my lips and said a prayer for the family's safety, then returned it to my pocket.

Three hours later, after a few slips and slides on the treacherous road, we arrived at Inuvik, meaning "place of people" in Inuktitut. With a fluctuating population of around 3,000, the settlement is situated on the east channel of the Mackenzie Delta. Only 224 feet above sea level, the area was developed as a result of oil exploration. The town became a supply center for petroleum company crews when the first well was drilled in 1965. The main engineering obstacle in building Inuvik was the deep permafrost, or frozen soil, which forced construction of water and sewer pipes above ground.

The Inuit, whose name means "the people," make up most of the town's population. They are no longer known as Eskimos, a disparaging term meaning "eaters of raw meat" that was attached to them by early white settlers. The culture of the Inuit, formerly nomadic hunters, has undergone radical changes over several generations. While much of the populace is generally welcoming and helpful, many Inuit consume huge quantities of alcohol. Late into the night, drunks weave their uncertain way from bar to bar. Their loud voices, often hurling profanities at no one in particular, echo through the snowy streets. Mornings are spent recovering in time to begin partying once more in the nighttime hours. Alcohol helps some get through the mind-numbing darkness of winter.

Whites, or *kabloona*, work in the government offices here and, as in other towns far above the Arctic Circle, seem out of place. Their culture does not suit life in the frozen north, forcing them to make major adjustments to cope with the intense cold and isolation.

Our first task in Inuvik was to contact John, who was eager to hear about our summer with the tundra wolves. He grew angry when we told him of the aerial hunters. "It's frustrating," he said. "The government just doesn't listen."

He had good news, though, about our prospects for finding wolves to observe. Just the day before, he had seen six wolves bedded down in sparse trees and willows about fifty miles across the delta, in a place far from snowmobile routes, where he had seen them sporadically for the last four years. He marked the place on our map with an X. Since first discovering the unusual habits of this wolf family, he had kept the location a closely guarded secret from his hunting friends.

In town throughout the day, the din of snowmobiles blasted the frigid air. The drivers, some in bright, neon-trimmed suits and helmets, appeared oblivious to everything except how fast they could go and how loud they could be. The noxious smell of fuel and ever-present plumes of blue smoke trailed behind them. To preserve life and limb, we quickly learned to listen for a roar before crossing a street. Although impressed by the drivers' abilities to swerve around us at the last possible moment, we were unimpressed by the choking exhaust. We much preferred the lifestyle of an expedition in the wilderness to the nerve-wracking stress of dodging traffic.

Poor Charlie was unhappy with the noise and commotion too. He jumped in alarm as yet another snowmobile sprayed him with dirty, gray street snow. We stayed in Inuvik only one day, just long enough to gather the last of our supplies—stove fuel and a few basics—and load our sleds. We had brought most of our food with us.

Our winter diet in continuous cold temperatures is one of carbohydrates and fats to maintain the warmth and energy needed to pull our heavy sleds. After dividing 360 pounds of food between the sleds, they each weighed 300 pounds. Based on our other Arctic expeditions, we planned a diet of 4,000 calories per day. In Inuvik we bought extra butter and several irresistible energy bars to add to our already generous stores, which included Charlie's favorite dog food and extra-protein treats, such as dried strips of chicken and beef. So that he would be free to walk at our sides, we carried his food on our sleds, just as we had carried his food in our packs last summer.

At Inuvik's northerly latitude the sunlight disappears for most of December, returns for a few minutes during the first week of January, and shows itself for several hours toward the end of the month. Due to darkness and our start in January, normally the coldest month of the year, we estimated that our approximately 350-mile round trip would take about thirty days in the gradually increasing daylight. To be on the safe side, we would carry supplies for fifty days, to last until mid-March.

John drove us to the banks of the frozen Mackenzie River outside of town, where the ice road leading to Tuk began. Each winter the river freezes with ice thick enough to drive on. Then snowplows clear away the surface snow to enable supply trucks and snowmobilers to drive the "highway" until the spring thaw reduces the delta to a giant mosquito-infested swamp.

A good morning stretch after being confined to the tent during our first arctic storm.

John helped us lift our loaded sleds from the pickup and waved good-bye. At last, with a sense of relief mixed with anticipation, we attached skis to our boots and sled harnesses to our waists and set forth on our winter expedition.

We were about to experience life in splendid solitude again, this time in the Mackenzie Delta and taiga forest, blanketed with snow and ice and locked in the depths of an arctic winter. We estimated that weather permitting, we would take six or seven days to cross the delta and arrive in Tuk, the only settlement along our route.

With Inuvik receding into the distance, Charlie returned to his cheerful self. He strode ahead with his normal impatient gait, signaling us to hurry. Our skis crunched against the dry, squeaky snow typical of the polar North. As we let go of Inuvik and our daily lives, our minds opened and peace prevailed as we looked ahead to life in a natural, simple space.

We gradually reoriented ourselves to a daily routine consisting mainly of the ebb and flow of weather, geography, and the snow beneath our feet. The *swish, swish* of our skis took the place of conversation. Our senses became more acute. Words were unnecessary as we listened to and watched nature slide by. Ptarmigan exploded from the snow around willow thickets, the heavy beat of their wings carrying them safely away from Charlie's lunges.

January's forbidding winter and monochromatic light contrasted with the softer hues we recalled from last summer's tundra environment. It was 36 degrees below zero. The sky was streaked with sun dogs, arcs of light the colors of a rainbow formed by ice crystals reflected in the sunlight. The slender spruce trees were Christmas-card perfect in their white cloaks. A snowy owl glided past in silent flight, its breath a thin stream of ice particles trailing behind. Three ravens flew by, their raucous voices loud and vaguely disturbing in the quiet.

Two months of tough, unrelenting training in the mountains had done much to acclimatize the three of us for the journey ahead, but it still took time to adjust to pulling a fully loaded sled and camping in subzero cold. At first our sleds felt like anchors around our hips. For the first two days, we followed the frozen ribbon of the East Channel of the Mackenzie River as it wound tortuously through stunted spruce.

Occasionally we passed items serving to mark the edges of the road—a barrel, a tall orange stake, a snowplow berm. As we stopped to allow three snowmobiles to pass, we looked forward to leaving the road and heading across the white landscape to make our own path. Charlie sneezed in the exhaust fumes and shook off the snow that landed on him as the Inuit snowmobilers accelerated past on bright red and yellow machines.

The immense delta, through which the Mackenzie River's contorted three main channels flow to the Beaufort Sea, is an ancient floodplain that developed during the retreat of the Wisconsin ice sheet thousands of years ago. Sluggish streams meander their way north through an elaborate mosaic of lakes and ponds. Stands of dwarf alder, birches, and willow are interspersed with low-growing sedges. Closer to the coast, most of the trees disappear and willow increases.

As we struggled along the ice road, I was reminded that in dry snow, sled runners do not slide as easily as they do in the wetter snow of Washington. With my load straining at my hips, I vaguely wondered at the wisdom of tossing aboard those extra energy bars. As the hours passed I resolved to have a generous dinner, topped off with as many of the bars as I could possibly eat. Tomorrow my sled would be lighter, I promised myself. It all sounded very familiar—reminiscent of my thoughts on many a previous journey, in fact. Meanwhile, Bill plodded steadily onward in his usual uncomplaining fashion.

As the first day progressed, feathery clouds signaled a weather change. We stopped for a late lunch of beef jerky, cashews, and walnuts, followed by a drink of hot chocolate. After gobbling half my beef jerky, Charlie turned his full attention to Bill and begged for more snacks. Only after he was soundly rebuffed did he eat his dog food.

The temperature rose to -29 degrees, but was still too cold to rest for more than ten minutes; any longer would allow the seeping cold to reach through our innermost layers. Next to our skin we wore thin thermal tops and pants. Next came a thick fleece sweater and pants, topped by a windproof, insulated hooded jacket. We also had a head-hugging fleece hat topped by a thermal, windproof outer hat. Our hands were covered with thin but warm glove liners under polar mitts, and our boots were especially designed for cold, dry climates. They were breathable, with rubber soles that gripped the snow and ice. Finally, neoprene masks protected our faces and warmed our breath before the searing cold could hit our lungs. Charlie, on the other hand, needed nothing but his thick black Arctic coat to keep warm.

As Bill and I skied along, each engrossed in our own thoughts, we exchanged places in the lead. Charlie mostly traveled at my side, but enjoyed taking an occasional turn with Bill. By midafternoon lenticular clouds, shaped like lenses and saucers, had developed to signal oncoming high winds.

Suddenly Bill called, "Moose to your right!"

An adult female browsed in the thick willow undergrowth. Remembering the summer episode when I had been chased by an angry mother, I froze. Charlie stared at the moose without moving. Now aware of us, she took a few quick steps, as though to flee, but changed her mind and continued browsing as she slowly wandered deeper into the entanglement. As she disappeared, Charlie stepped ahead to continue the journey as though nothing unusual had happened.

In late afternoon's rapidly fading light, more lenticular clouds billowed across the sky. The rising wind ripped through the treetops, sending a full-scale storm bearing down on us. We rushed to erect the tent. Within ten minutes and with perfect teamwork, we anchored it securely and tossed our gear inside, just as a blizzard began to hurtle snow in horizontal blasts that we estimated at sixty miles per hour. Bill and I both dived in headfirst, followed by Charlie. I lunged at the door zipper, pulled it shut, and leaned back, panting.

"Whew!" I said. "Just in time."

Charlie lay back in comfort. We rearranged our gear, ready to wait out a storm that could last days. After the sleeping bags and equipment were in place, we cooked a dinner of soup and crackers followed by dehydrated rice and vegetables with butter added to increase calories. Dessert was an easy decision: energy bars.

At the beginning of an expedition, the food always seems quite tasty. As time passes, especially in cold climates, it reduces itself to the taste of sawdust as cold numbs taste buds and the same fare appears over and over. To keep our loads as light as possible and to simplify cooking, we ate the same nutritious, energy-laden items each day with little variation, supplementing them with multivitamins and extra vitamin C.

Lest our spirits become defeated by the tedious diet, we never critique the food while traveling. Allowing our minds to wander to thoughts of more varied, mouthwatering fare does not help our resolve to continue onward. And persistence and dedication to the task ahead is sometimes all that keeps us going through the difficult stretches of sled hauling.

After dinner we climbed into our down sleeping bags, far more heavy-duty than our lightweight summer models. All night the wind roared and snow dumped on our tiny home. Now and then we beat the inside walls to knock down the snow that rapidly built up outside, particularly on the windward side. By first light, late the next morning, the storm had lessened its fury, but it strengthened again by midday. To stay warm, we remained in our sleeping bags. Charlie, spread across my bag as usual, took up more and more room as time went on, until I was forced to push him off and start over. I again claimed a generous share that I knew would gradually disappear.

After two feet of windblown snow had built up on one side of the tent, we had no choice but to venture outside to clear it away lest the wall collapse. The shock of the cold wind forced us to work at top speed. The sleds were buried, but at least they wouldn't blow away. Finished, we plunged into the tent, this time taking a large amount of snow with us. Charlie looked up, stretched, and yawned. Bill and I brushed snow off each other's backs and then, after stowing our boots in the vestibule, retreated into the depths of our warm sleeping bags.

We emerged to brave the elements only reluctantly, to attend to toilet duties. Again the cold made speed essential. Charlie woke us up twice to go outside, scratching at the tent door. By dinnertime the storm had subsided, but it was too dark to pack and start skiing. We cooked dinner, snuggled deep into the folds of our warm sleeping bags, and slept soundly.

The next day the first light of breaking dawn crept silently through the spruce trees. The storm had passed, leaving us to wallow in deep drifts of snow. In the gray silence that followed the storm, we ate a quick breakfast of oatmeal, milk powder, and dried fruit, then dressed to dig out the sleds. The wind had blasted the snow into hollows and ridges, some as high as three feet. As the skies cleared, the temperature dropped to -45 degrees. We packed and headed north.

To make up for lost time, we pulled at a steady pace. I had looked forward to a lighter sled after eating our first day's food and burning fuel in our stove. But the effect of the slightly lighter load was more than cancelled out by the resistance of the layer of new snow over the ice. Even stoic Bill was heard to complain. We camped in the late afternoon under moonlight.

The next day we left the ice road and headed cross-country. We knew that sled hauling across the roadless terrain would be more difficult, but escaping the rumbling supply trucks and snowmobiles was our reward. To avoid the trees and other vegetation, we followed a meandering route across frozen lakes and twisting channels. The flat surfaces allowed us to make good time in the clear weather. We wondered, as we skirted patches of gnarled trees, how long these pitiful specimens, ripped and blasted by Arctic storms, had taken to reach their ten-foot height. Although far from the majestic size of trees found in southern forests, some white spruce in the delta have been documented to be 560 years old. They were probably here when the river was first discovered by Scottish explorer Alexander Mackenzie and his men in 1789.

Several white arctic foxes scurried away from a dark mound in the snow as we skied across a miniature lake. We investigated and found half the body of a female moose. Judging by the ripped abdomen, the animal had been killed by wolves, perhaps that morning, although none were in evidence now. Wolf pawprints and the smaller prints of foxes surrounded the body. We guessed that the wolves either had eaten their fill and moved on, or were resting somewhere and would return to finish their feast. Meanwhile, the foxes were taking advantage of the fresh kill. Already we had found more evidence of one animal's hunting skills benefiting another.

After a few days our bodies had adjusted to the daily grind of hauling sleds, setting up camp, making dinner, sleeping, and beginning all over again the next morning. We had a new appreciation for the luxury of last summer, when we had camped in one place close to the den and never had to search for wolves.

In still weather the delta is a silent place, everything frozen, waiting for spring's release from the icy prison. The biting cold made it difficult to imagine how it might look in summer, when it is the watery home for a wide variety of nesting birds such as tundra swans, geese, golden plovers, sandhill cranes, and willow ptarmigan, as well as black clouds of mosquitoes.

Almost halfway to Tuk on day six another storm swept through, this time bringing strong gales from the south. We made good time with the wind at our backs, pushing us along. The gray sky blended with the far-off horizon, turning colors to black and white. The weak sun that hid somewhere in the cold sky made depth perception tricky as the shadows disappeared. Windblown snow scurried along the rock-hard surface, passing us in long streamers. Now and then we stumbled when we hit bumps and holes that were invisible in the flat light.

Once, as we skied down a shallow hollow, I slipped and fell. My sled didn't stop until it knocked me off my feet. An amused Bill laughed to see me on my back on the snow and my sled halfway on top. As he helped me to my feet I informed him, in icy tones that easily matched our surroundings, that I failed to see the humor in my being run over by my own sled. He stopped laughing, but I could see a twinkle in his eye. Charlie calmly observed the entire episode, no doubt wondering why I could not stay on my feet, as it was never a problem for him.

We spent three days waiting for another storm to pass, then set out to cross a snowy moonscape. We soon learned to avoid the hollows, which were traps waiting to bog down our sleds. By now the weather and soft snow had dropped us far behind schedule. It was day twelve. At our present pace we were at least three days from Tuk, but our supply of food was plentiful. Arctic foxes scurried by. Moose and caribou looked up as we passed. More wolf tracks crisscrossed those of arctic foxes, but still we saw no wolves.

Charlie treated each wild animal differently. The ptarmigan left him unimpressed—birds just did not count—but the foxes deserved special attention. He leaped to the end of his leash in fake charges that usually made the foxes scurry away, but some sat and stared, as if to tease him. They knew his tether would stop him. The moose were a more serious business. Charlie watched them as he would a polar bear, sensing their mood, to judge whether he should become a growling, menacing ball of fury or wait quietly, body tense and ready. Because he so loved chasing wild animals, we kept him leashed at our side most of the time, not only for his own safety but to prevent the local wild inhabitants from becoming nervous as we skied past.

Several miles south of Tuk, evidence of recent kills lay in the bloody patches of snow and tufts of fur strewn about, leaving the story of the hunt to our imagination. Although the wolves had remained invisible so far, we knew they were close. Charlie enthusiastically left his mark and tried to follow the tracks. He was deeply disappointed by our uncooperative attitude.

The thick willow brush and deep snowdrifts challenged us. Our sleds developed the maddening habit of jamming in the willows. Repeatedly, we had to push and pull them free. It was exhausting work for all three of us. Even Charlie had problems finding solid surfaces in the snow. I unleashed him so he could make his way around the worst hollows. But with his broad chest paving the way, he could power through the deepest drifts.

On February 3, the fifteenth day of our trek, we reached the outskirts of Tuk, having been much delayed by storms and soft snow. The town was a dark smudge of low buildings amid the white glare of winter. A settlement of about 1,000 residents, Tuk is Canada's northern base for gas and oil exploration in the Beaufort Sea. The town's future is doubtful, however. Scientists are concerned that due to global warming the permafrost is melting and the sea is devouring the coastline at a rate of about six feet per year. Attempts to block the waves have so far been unsuccessful and the town's inhabitants face the possibility of relocating to higher ground far inland.

In the shelter of our tent, we discussed plans over dinner. Should we venture into Tuk or continue with our original plan? Tired of snowmobiles, we decided to skirt the settlement and head straight for the sea ice. We sealed the pledge with a double-strength hot chocolate and hugged Charlie, who gently licked our faces in agreement.

The next morning we left at first light. The lengthening days allowed us to travel longer hours. To stay off steep banks and entangled willow thickets, we followed a lengthy path over the frozen river channels twisting toward the coast.

Tuk is surrounded by numerous pingos—huge, permanent hills with a core of ice that grow only in permafrost. ("Pingo," an Inuktitut word, simply means "conical hill.") Pingos can reach heights of more than a hundred feet and form when an ice mound pushes upward, taking a layer of vegetation with it. There are more than 1,500 pingos in the Mackenzie Delta. Some resemble Egyptian pyramids, while the smaller ones look like volcanic cones. One of the world's largest, called Ibyuk, is reputed to be 160 feet high and 1,000 feet wide and is located a few miles southwest of Tuk. Several species of birds, especially rough-legged hawks, nest in the vegetation-covered slopes.

The next day as Bill, Charlie, and I wound back and forth along the river channels, the thought of the sea ice and wolves ahead urged us onward. At one point we followed three sets of wolf tracks but still saw no wolves.

At midday we reached the coast and the windblown, relatively snow-free ice that provided long-sought relief to our tiring bodies. Just as we neared the icy Beaufort Sea, two white wolves crossed our path only a few hundred feet ahead. One male carried a large chunk of seal, and his female companion carried a smaller portion. Charlie tensed. The pair stopped momentarily to look at us, then trotted westward.

Within minutes a lone male, also carrying part of a seal, loped across the ice, hurrying to catch the first two. The encounter was so different from our first meeting with Alpha and his family, who had watched us with intense suspicion as we neared their den. These sea ice wolves barely paused to notice us as they hurried to some distant place to eat their meal. Apparently the wolves had found an abandoned polar bear kill and shared in the bounty.

After pushing our way through the snow and ice for sixteen days, we were thrilled. Our quest to observe wolves, polar bears, and their hunting habits on the sea ice had begun.

Bears

T HE ROUGH COASTAL ICE of the Beaufort Sea was a precarious jumble of massive slabs and blocks, strewn about as if thrown by a giant. It creaked and groaned as we pulled our sleds farther out onto its frozen surface.

Charlie was delighted to be on sea ice again, which he had loved on previous northern expeditions. Once we cleared the unstable shore jumble, he rolled for a luxurious back scratch, all four feet in the air, wriggling back and forth with contented grunts.

When the sea first freezes, the surface is covered with a layer of fine crystals resembling an oily film. The crystals join and thicken into a layer of gray, salty slush that rises and falls with the gentle swells. As ice ages and thickens, the salt gradually drops, turning the surface into white, freshwater ice that can be melted for cooking and drinking water.

Pack ice, or multiyear ice, covers most of the open polar sea. It continues to harden and thicken to sometimes more than fifty feet. Ocean currents and storm winds keep the ice in constant motion, changing its shape into long ridges of dangerous teetering blocks and vast areas of rubble. When winds and currents split the surface, the edges drift away from each other. In violent storms the sections can move half a mile apart, forming a gaping water chasm.

In previous expeditions, we had spent hours and sometimes days waiting for the water to refreeze or for edges to join together. Two words describe polar sea ice: unpredictable and dangerous.

As our sleds glided easily across the thin layer of snow covering the ice, we skied a course over the frozen sea, away from Tuk and toward Pullen Island, which lay fifty-two miles and about five days to the northwest. Here we found no mysterious green valleys, narrow caribou trails, or new spring growth pushing up toward the sun, as we had on our way to the summer den. Instead we faced an endless crumpled ice sheet that stretched into a blue infinity. We imagined ourselves leaving the world behind as we headed toward the polar ice cap. There would be no wolf family at their den. Any wolves here would be scattered across the ice, and our task was to find them.

Later that day we reached an uneven area of twenty-foot-high ridges split by narrow gaps, the chaos a result of storms and the Mackenzie River. As the river flows into the sea in the dropping fall temperatures, the river current, although sluggish, moves the setting ice in all directions, creating an obstacle course of ridges and rubble. Immediately off the coast, because of the silt-laden river flow, the water depth is only a few feet in places.

The head-on tactics we had used on previous Arctic expeditions through ice ridges worked this time as well. We hauled our sleds behind us by hand and dropped them down the other side of each ridge as we struggled over the top. Charlie, meanwhile, leaped nimbly from block to block with perfect balance. The extraordinarily clear air provided brilliant visibility as we peered through the white glare, hoping to see a smoother path ahead. But the miles of jumbled ice stretched on and on.

Just as I pulled my sled through a tight gap that almost jammed it, the ice suddenly groaned as it settled and moved with the sea currents. Blocks, some the size of small cars, toppled as if they were toys. The ice was on the move.

Bill yelled, "Leave the sleds and get out!"

Two male bears growl mouth to mouth, testing each other over hunting space.

Dropping my sled harness, I scrambled down just as another great groan rumbled through the ice, toppling even more blocks. Charlie leaped the gaps to follow close at my heels. From the relative safety of a flat ice pan, we watched the sleds sway among the unstable blocks that threatened to crush them. After fifteen minutes, there was silence.

We scrambled back to our sleds, praying that the ice wouldn't move. We grabbed the sled ropes, jerked the sleds free, and hauled them down to flat ice. No sooner were we convinced that things had settled down than we heard a deep rumbling. Quick as lightning, a split opened ten feet behind us. With a rush of adrenaline we dashed in the opposite direction, toward what looked like stable ice. Huge cracks cut through the surface at our heels as we ran. One suddenly appeared three feet ahead. We hurdled it, still dragging our sleds.

The sound had grown to thunderous proportions. All around us, the unstable pack still moved. Terrified, we ran a half mile before the vibration and roaring subsided enough to allow us to stop, out of breath, wondering if we might still be chewed up in the jaws of the breaking ice.

As we regained our breath, the untamed sounds of raw nature faded away. The crisis had passed. We were still in one piece. We hugged each other and Charlie with relief.

There was enough daylight left to escape the precarious area before nightfall. We turned east in search of a safe route and encountered day-old polar bear paw prints mixed with the smaller tracks of arctic foxes. As Charlie caught the bear scent, he tugged at his leash, urging us to follow the tracks. "Forget it, Charlie," I said. "We've got more important things to do." After I gave a determined pull on his leash, he reluctantly gave up the idea.

Two hours later and six miles out of our way, we reached the end of the ridge and could see level ice stretching several miles northwest. To celebrate, we stopped to eat a quick snack. With the temperature down to -41 degrees, we resisted the temptation to stay long. Even though the sounds of the ice breakup had faded, the many splits and gaps we continued to cross reminded us of the trauma we had escaped. Hurdling three-foot-wide splits with long jumps and quick pulls, we skied ahead to find a safe campsite. It wasn't until the gray dusk closed in that we stopped. With cold fingers and tired bodies we made camp, relieved to end the day's hard travel. Now that we were camping on ice we anchored our tent with mountaineering ice screws, hollow, six-inch titanium tubes that screwed into the ice.

At daybreak, after a restful night, we sat in our sleeping bags eating a hot breakfast of oatmeal and dried fruit while we studied our map. Yesterday's long detour still left us forty-nine miles from Pullen Island.

Although the air outside was a frigid -33 degrees, the good visibility and smooth ice made skiing easier, with a only few easy ups and downs to traverse. But the sun's glare reflecting off the ice tortured our eyes. Our goggles fogged up all morning. We had to raise them frequently to see, and by afternoon the brightness began to burn our eyes. It was a relief to close them that night.

For the next two days we regularly crossed polar bear, wolf, and fox tracks, all traveling from one seal breathing hole to another. Judging by the patches of blood and tiny scraps of seal hide on the ice, the bears had made several kills. The abundant seal population guaranteed good hunting for the polar bears, who always sensed where the best seal hunting grounds were.

The breathing holes of ringed seals, or *natiq*, were places of delight for Charlie, with delightful seal aromas and occasionally even a few scraps of meat, which he chewed with gusto. We couldn't persuade him to leave any hole until he had properly inspected it, licked up all the blood, and eaten every scrap of meat and hide.

We kept a careful 360-degree lookout for bears. Our loaded shotguns lay on top of our sleds alongside the flare guns and several dozen flares. As we traveled through an area of ice pinnacles high enough to hide a waiting bear, we mostly relied on Charlie's acute sense of hearing and smell to warn us of any trouble.

One day after two hours of zigzagging we finally skied onto smoother ice, rounding a six-foot pile of ice rubble. Dead ahead rested a polar bear and her two cubs. A hundred feet away Charlie stopped, watched quietly for a moment, and then led us away, knowing the bear wouldn't approach as long as we skied onward.

Without pausing we continued, as unhurriedly as we could, hoping not to leave the impression that we were running away, which could invite the mother to chase us. With her cubs tucked firmly to her furry side, she remained still. The cubs, born the previous spring, were dependent on their mother, who would nurture them for their first two years. An arctic fox scampered

Charlie whips around to face the bear and leaps,
snarling in our defense.

across our path with hardly a glance in our direction as he carried a foot-long chunk of sealskin left over from a bear kill.

An hour later we met another bear and cubs. This mother
immediately moved protectively ahead of her two offspring,
who cautiously peeked from her side. She growled. Charlie
sensed her aggression. She took a second step forward as her
growls grew angry. He responded with mouth-frothing snarls as
he leaped to the end of his leash. She turned with her cubs close
to her side and, running with the polar bear's typical pigeon-
toed gait, disappeared into the chaotic ice.

Later we sighted two distant polar bears being followed by a
wolf, his dark coat easily visible against the glare. Scattered
mounds of ice reflected pastel blue and green as we moved
through the frozen landscape. Soft colors, framed by white, surrounded us. A perfect Arctic day.

Two hours before dark we camped, still within sight of the hunting bears and wolf. Charlie, who continued to keep watch, caught an array of smells on the gentle breeze. He was in his element, staring across the ice at the bears. One leaped into the water but returned without a seal. In anticipation of the bear's successful dive, the wolf leaned over the edge of the ice but trotted across to the second bear when he saw that the first had been unsuccessful.

Just as Charlie was about to turn his full attention to his food bowl, he suddenly whipped around to face the rear and leaped, snarling, to the end of his leash. To our horror, a bear emerged from head-high hummocks of ice three hundred feet away. He was striding straight toward us.

Charlie's snarls reached a fierce crescendo. We grabbed our loaded flare guns and rapidly fired several flares to land on the ice in front of the advancing bear. But he marched right through the first line. We reloaded and fired. He didn't stop. We each grabbed a shotgun and released the safety catches, still firing more flares. The bear stopped, raised his nose to test the thin curtain of flare smoke, and shook his head. Disturbed by the unfamiliar smell, he slowly backed away.

Charlie strained at the end of his leash in a frenzied rage. Apparently, Charlie and the smoke were too much for the bear. He turned and walked around us, defiantly tossing a look back over his shoulder as if he might return. But Charlie, who still leaped and snarled, discouraged him.

While I collected the empty casings and tossed them into our plastic garbage bag, Bill stood guard with his shotgun to make sure that our unwanted visitor had indeed left and would not double back. Eventually Charlie calmed down, but he remained vigilant for another hour, staring in the direction the bear had gone. We cautiously resumed our interrupted meal. Tonight the bear would have to look for his own dinner elsewhere.

The next day, after a blissfully bear-free night, we traveled over a minor ridge and skied across smooth ice. We reached an area of ice mounds molded and sculptured by nature into shapes delicately curved and tinted green with age. They reached upward to stand like sentinels, guarding the way ahead. Later the surface smoothed to a uniform whiteness, snow and clouds merging into one at the horizon.

At midday we arrived at an area of open water several hundred yards wide. Six seal-hunting polar bears were pacing the edges, followed by five wolves and numerous foxes who dodged in and out, careful to keep out of range of their larger companions. Two male bears growled nose to nose, testing each other over hunting space. We camped close by, reasoning that the animals were too busy searching for seals to notice us. We ate cold food so our noisy stove wouldn't mask the sound of an approaching bear.

A few years earlier, during a training expedition close to Resolute Bay, we had encountered thirteen bears striding along the edges of sea ice hunting for seals, accompanied by four wolves. We nervously skirted the area. We weren't prepared to meet that many bears in one place. Now, more experienced, we felt cautiously comfortable, although we continued to keep a sharp eye out and our shotguns and flare guns at hand.

Back at the water, one large male hovered over a patch of ice, several feet from the edge. Suddenly he rose on his hind legs and crashed down with enormous front paws to land his full weight over a seal lair. The ice broke. He thrust his head through the opening, yanked out a struggling seal, and dumped it on the ice. In seconds he had crushed the seal's head and torn off thick strips of blubber.

A sixth wolf, with a gray-tinted blond coat and a large dark patch on one rump, stood a few feet away. Occasionally the bear growled a warning to the wolf not to approach his meal. After he had consumed the blubber, the fatty part of the seal, the bear left the meaty carcass and returned to the water's edge. The wolf immediately claimed the body while foxes scampered just out of reach, waiting for leftovers. Thirty minutes later, after the wolf had gorged himself, he left the skeleton and meat scraps for the half-dozen foxes.

Wolves' normal habitat is land, where their natural prey of caribou and moose are available. Wolves and foxes are not the natural swimmers that polar bears are, so they cannot hunt seals in the water. They also lack the weight and power to break the ice to reach seal lairs.

We were now beginning to understand how wolves survived on the ice. Polar bears appeared to be the key. We had observed wolves and foxes following as the bears hunted seals, waiting for a kill. The smaller animals cleverly allowed the bears to do the hunting, while they scavenged the leftovers. We theorized that after the sea ice was strong enough to provide a hunting platform for the bears, those wolves who travel with bears left the land for the sea ice and followed the bears as they hunted.

We watched the hunting activities until dark. Although the blond wolf, whom we called Patch because of his rump mark, seemed to prefer working alone, he joined the other five occasionally. Once, as he approached his companions, they all ran in tight circles. It seemed to be a game in which everyone chased everyone else. In minutes they stopped, joined in an enthusiastic display of muzzle licking, then rejoined the bears to see what was being offered for dinner. We wondered if these were members of a single family.

After dark, as a precaution against bears, we slept in two-hour shifts, with Bill taking the first watch. During my turn I stepped into the sharp air, a chilly -31 degrees. I pulled my bulky down parka around me and tucked my hands deeper into my polar gloves. The moonlight reflecting on the ice enabled me to see animals moving about at night. Now and then the ice spoke its own special language: cracking sounds, long humanlike sighs, and a peculiar whine that built to a frenzied pitch before sliding back down the scale to silence. The immense frozen ocean was protesting its imprisonment, I imagined, as the ice moved with the ocean currents.

I felt very alone as I stood on guard. In the gray darkness, my world had shrunk. Pinnacles of ice, impossibly tall in the deceptive light, loomed against the starry sky. I looked to my left, straining to penetrate the dim surroundings. Was it my imagination, or did I really detect a slight movement in the distance?

I was reminded of my solo trek to the magnetic North Pole and of the many times I stood outside my tent trying to see through the darkness, hoping a polar bear wasn't watching and licking his lips in anticipation of a tasty meal. I don't mind traveling alone, even when faced with polar bears, dangerous ice, and storms. Along with vulnerability comes a mind-opening effect, an elation caused by a sharpened awareness as my senses become more acute. It's a time when I feel completely in step with nature.

But I'm always thankful to travel with Bill. We know each other so well that we can often tell what the other is thinking even before words are spoken. It's a comfort to express fears to someone. Daily tasks, such as navigating and bear watching, are simplified. And camp chores such as erecting the tent are quick and easy when the two of us work together and draw upon each other's strengths.

I tried to keep my nerves at bay, but nevertheless my anxiety built. *No,* I thought, *it's your imagination. Nothing's moving out there.* At one point Charlie joined me with hackles raised, his body tense and on guard. He stared into the distance, sensing a bear, and I braced myself and reached for the shotgun. But I saw nothing, and nothing happened.

After thirty minutes Charlie gave a low, sharp *woof* and disappeared into the tent. I both marveled at and envied his instinctive ability to sense bears, and was thankful for his cease-less desire to keep Bill and me safe.

Later, on his watch, Bill caught sight of a far-off bear and a wolf traveling together to the water's edge. Charlie stepped out of the tent, but this time, after a short, intense stare at the ghostly forms, he relaxed and, without a sound, returned to bed. The bear's intentions were peaceful, and Charlie understood.

Morning crept slowly across the ice, and with it came the blessed relief of good visibility. The bears had hunted through-out the night. We weren't surprised that day and night were the same to these sea ice hunters. During the summer Denali had led his family on many successful nighttime hunts, especially as temperatures rose, making daytime hunting less attractive.

We stayed another day to watch the activities. With a great splash a bear dived into the water and surfaced with a young seal. After the bear climbed onto the ice, he consumed most of the blubber before turning back to the water's edge to await fur-ther opportunities. Two wolves rushed to devour the rest of the

Dead ahead is a mother with two cubs.

seal. They left to follow the bears only after licking the blood-stains from the ice. Throughout the day the bears hunted, and the waiting wolves and foxes shared the leftovers.

Later a large, blond male wolf approached the water. He was followed by a smaller, limping female of slightly darker coloring. She appeared to have injured a front paw. Meanwhile, a massive bear with three wolves waiting at a respectful distance stood over a seal breathing hole. Two wolves were almost identical in their gray coats. One had a dried blood smudge on his shoulder but no other sign of injury, so we surmised it was from a seal car-cass. The third wolf, slightly smaller, had a peculiar crablike gait as he ran across the ice, so we named him Crab.

Just as the female and blond male arrived, the bear thrust his head into the seal hole he had been standing over for at least a half hour. He hauled out a thrashing seal, crushed its head and, without stopping to eat, walked to the edge of the ice and stared into the water. The three wolves accompanying him wasted no time rushing to the body. Several foxes dashed in and out in short spurts, barely keeping out of reach of the snapping jaws as they grabbed small pieces.

While two of the wolves gorged themselves, the third one, the one with the smudge on his shoulder, tore off a large chunk of meat and delivered it to the blond male, who had stopped fifty feet away. After dropping the meat to the ice, he turned back to the seal. Meanwhile, the female had limped closer. Without taking a single bite, her blond companion took the meat to her. She hungrily grabbed it and gulped it down. Her companion turned back to the three wolves, and as he approached them, the same wolf who had provided him with the gift of meat, whom we named Smudge, once more took a large portion and dropped it at the blond wolf's feet. Blondy, as we now called him, chomped down the lot of it, while the other wolves finished off the rest of the carcass.

It appeared that food had been deliberately provided by the polar bear. The wolves had shared it among themselves and had divided it so that even the injured female could eat. We surmised that the female and Blondy might have been a bonded pair, while Smudge, who had delivered the meat, was probably an alpha taking care of all the members of his family.

Fascinated, we continued to watch. After the carcass disappeared, the first three wolves again shadowed the bear as he stalked the water's edge a quarter mile to the north. Blondy stayed with the female, as if to help her, and both remained within easy distance of their companions, as if to await further gifts of food. The episode reminded us of the attention given to Beta after he injured himself during the summer, and of the many times food was placed at his side by his caring family.

The process captivated us. Polar bears, the primary hunters, killed the prey and then ate mostly the fat. Wolves and foxes then shared the meat. During several years of Arctic travels, this was the first time we had actually seen this sequence of events, although for some time we had suspected it existed. The large number of bears and wolves we encountered was unusual, due no doubt to the open water and plentiful seal population, creating a perfect hunting ground.

Soon it was too dark to see more. The next morning we looked out at first light, but the bear and all the wolves had moved on.

Ice

STILL WITH NO ANIMALS IN SIGHT and many miles to go, we packed up in the last gray light of dawn and trekked in the direction of Richards and Pullen Islands, both named for early Arctic explorers who helped map the northern Canadian coastline. For several hours we skied with the distant outline of Richards Island to the west. Tiny Pullen Island was still invisible farther north in the Beaufort Sea, well into the western Northwest Passage.

As we approached a twenty-foot-high pyramid of sparkling blue ice, Charlie stopped and yipped several times. Puzzled because the sound was different from his usual bear-warning bark, we allowed him to pull us around to the other side.

We froze, astonished. Two hundred feet away was a group of eleven wolves, all of whom we had seen on and off since leaving land. Smudge, whose behavior now confirmed that he was a family alpha, had already detected our approach. Stiff-legged, hostile, lips pulled back in a snarl, he stood in front of his family, ready to defend them.

Close behind him, the limping female hurried to join Blondy, who shielded her protectively. The others, including Crab and Patch, watched and paced nervously, never taking their eyes off us. Charlie squatted on his haunches, while Bill and I hastily sat on our sleds and looked away to show that we weren't a threat. Then Smudge and Blondy joined in a series of barks in varying tones, interspersed with growls through bared teeth, designed to keep us away.

Charlie dropped to his belly with his muzzle averted, touching the ice. Led by Smudge, the entire family abruptly galloped another hundred feet away to cluster behind two foot-high chunks of ice, then turned to watch us suspiciously. We slowly rose, turned our sleds and, with Charlie at our side, retreated the way we had come, swinging wide onto open, flat ice. Although we were now farther away, we still had an easy view of the family. Once again we sat on our sleds while Charlie lay on his belly on the ice, his head half-turned away in submission.

We had disturbed the group as they rested in a place they frequented regularly, judging by the many patches of urine-discolored snow and the numerous wolf scats nearby. After a fifteen-minute standoff the wolves, although still cautious, relaxed their stiff-legged posture. Smudge barked a short warning with no sign of his earlier bared teeth and growling. Charlie, still belly down on the ice, raised his head and replied with yips so soft even we understood they were benevolent.

At first there was a long silence. Perhaps Smudge was trying to judge this black, doglike wolf offering friendship. Then he replied with a few gentle yips, the last one ending on a penetratingly high note. The group gathered about their leader in a tight bunch, and he calmly led them away. They disappeared into an area of rough ice to the north. The limping female easily kept up, her limp barely perceptible.

As they turned away, Charlie stood and tried to follow until his leash stopped him. With a tug, he urged us forward. "No, Charlie, not this time," I said quietly, as we headed west toward Pullen Island.

Meeting the sea ice wolves as a family answered a question that had increasingly bothered us. Why were we encountering so many wolves in a place where we would have considered ourselves lucky to see one or two? Even in our most optimistic mood, we had never imagined discovering an entire family.

We judged this spot to be a temporary resting site used by these wolves when open leads of water provided hunting bears with access to the area. Once the leads froze or shut, the bears would move to another area of open water, and the wolves would follow. Just as Alpha would be leading his pack across the southern tundra throughout the winter to hunt over a wide range, Smudge was leading his family on a journey across the frozen ocean. They had cleverly discovered that hunting was easier if they followed bears and shared whenever they could.

During the spring ice melt, the wolf family would be forced to abandon the ice and return to land. If a female was pregnant, they would dig a den or return to an old one, just as the summer wolves had done. The wolves in this pack, generally much lighter in color than Alpha's family, were about the same individual size. Smudge exhibited total control of his group as he led them to safety, his proud and imposing bearing reminding us of Alpha.

A shadowless fog swirled about us as we neared Richards Island, slowing our progress to a blind crawl. We could scarcely see our outstretched hands. Depth perception had disappeared. We drifted in a silent void where east and west, north and south, up and down were all the same. Slowly we moved in what we hoped was the right direction, gambling that our ski tips wouldn't drop into a watery abyss. The islands lay somewhere ahead, we thought. Engulfed in white, I stopped and shook my head to rid myself of a wave of vertigo.

"I hardly know whether I'm standing up straight," Bill said, straining to see ahead. "I feel as if I'm floating."

In our diminutive ice world, where we could see no more than a foot in any direction, each step was an adventure, like walking on a cloud. Even the ice underfoot was obscured by fog. We stumbled in the hollows and tripped on raised chunks of ice.

When I belatedly checked our direction on my compass, I discovered that instead of traveling northwest, we were skiing

Charlie rests while we set up camp on the sea ice.

due south. We had traveled in a circle and were headed back toward land. I was leading and had made the foolish mistake of assuming that I knew the right direction. Bill kindly remained silent as I slipped the compass into a holder at my waist to make it easier to stay on course.

"I hope polar bears don't like fog and stay home," I said nervously. More than ever, we would have to rely on Charlie to warn us.

An elated Charlie picked up the scent of polar bear tracks. He pulled out all the stops, with all manner of yips and tugging on his leash, to persuade us to follow the scent, but we insisted on a northerly course, away from trouble. He reluctantly agreed, but dropped back to follow on our heels with head and tail down to show his displeasure. After a half mile he was in front again, though, his gait buoyant and confident, his gaze ahead intense. No doubt he was hoping for more bear scents and sightings, while we were hoping all the area's bears were many miles distant.

We half-expected a bear to emerge suddenly from the ghostly fog as we skied slowly ahead. Twice Charlie halted us on the edges of cracks several feet wide. In the whiteout we couldn't see them, but he sensed the open water in time to stop. We groped our way around detours onto solid footing, thankful Charlie was along to save us from falling into unseen water.

Seven nerve-wracking hours later, our boots crunched across thin coastal ice. In a world still no more than two feet wide, our GPS unit faithfully confirmed our position: We had arrived at the northernmost tip of tiny Pullen Island. Judging by the fragile ice underfoot, we had practically gone ashore.

We peered into the swirling whiteness at something long and bleached white. Further investigation showed the object to be a weather-beaten log. At first it made no sense in that tree-less place. Then we remembered that logs from southern forests float down the Mackenzie River. Upon reaching the Beaufort Sea, swift ocean currents sweep them west until Arctic storms cast them onto the northern shores.

We retreated to more stable ice to set up camp as dusk darkened our claustrophobic world. We were relieved to escape into our tent, where we could look at something besides the blank whiteness of the fog.

There was no wind. For once the ice was still. Before sliding into our sleeping bags for the night, we checked outside but could see nothing. Alone in the Arctic darkness, I felt a brooding mood descend upon our tent. I wondered aloud whether the bears would be kind enough to keep their distance tonight.

"No use worrying about them when we can't do much about it," said Bill.

"Well, I'm not going to allow them to ruin a good night's sleep," I said. I definitely did not want to sleep in two-hour shifts as we had before. Bill and I are both day people, and I always found it particularly difficult to stay awake during night watches.

Even the threat of polar bears was sometimes not sufficient to keep me awake. Bill claimed that I fell asleep on my feet.

Although troubled by the fog and bears, we rested well for the first two hours. But then Charlie suddenly rose and listened at the door. Bill opened the zipper, which sounded loud in the perfectly still night. Perhaps Charlie needed to relieve himself, I thought, but he didn't move. His head turned to his right, then slowly moved to his left, as though following something unseen.

We had learned long ago to respect Charlie's reactions around bears. Now we remained quiet, although my pounding heart felt as though it was about to leap out of my chest. My brain silently screamed, *Is there a bear out there?* Both Bill and I carefully reached for our shotguns. In cold climates, we don't keep firearms in the tent. Any condensation in the firing mechanism would freeze, rendering the weapon useless. Instead we leave our guns in the cold vestibule, with a portion of the butt barely inside the door. We made slits in the door at floor level for just this purpose.

After five or ten minutes that seemed like forever, Charlie relaxed. His tail fanned back and forth, and after two yips he spread himself out on my sleeping bag with a contented sigh to resume his sleep. The episode was over for him, but we, still clutching our shotguns, continued to listen to the deep silence and its echoes in our imaginations.

Soon, though, the biting cold sent us back to our sleeping bags. "It had to be a bear. But Charlie seemed to send a friendly signal," Bill whispered, as though afraid any noise might attract an unwelcome guest.

I agreed, still feeling exposed and vulnerable to whatever had caught Charlie's attention. We were puzzled by his friendly reaction, which was more in keeping with greeting a wolf than a polar bear.

Sleep came only fitfully for the rest of the night. Dawn greeted us with the same silent mist. Hoping it might lift, we waited. But after several of the most boring hours of the expedition had passed, there was no improvement. At least in a storm we could listen to the wind. Here the only sound was the cracking of the ice pack as it moved. After a short discussion, we decided to begin our trip back to the mainland and hope conditions would clear. Although sorry to miss seeing Richards and Pullen Islands up close, we felt unsafe lingering amid so many bears.

As I loaded my sleeping bag onto the sled, I looked down. Right beside the runners was a large set of polar bear paw prints and two sets of wolf tracks that continued right past our tent, only three feet in front of the door. Now the nighttime picture was clear. When Charlie had listened so intently he must have known there was a bear outside, but his yips had been a greeting to the two wolves following the bear.

Bill agreed, but wondered just how far the bear had traveled and in which direction. Might he still be nearby? Charlie showed no sign of scenting a bear, but Bill was taking no chances. "Just in case they didn't go far, let's get out of here," he said.

We packed our sleds in record time, attached skis to boots, buckled our harnesses around our waists, and set off. Movement might give us a false sense of security, but it was better than contemplating a dubious future in the claws and jaws of a hungry polar bear.

Charlie displayed no such fear. His calm demeanor embarrassed us as we hurried away from the ghostly forms we imagined in the fog. He walked placidly ahead of me, knowing all was well and perhaps wishing his humans would get a grip on their emotions.

As we followed the compass needle southeast, leaving the shoreline of the island, the fog continued to thicken. The presence of bears and heavy fog made us suspect there was a much larger expanse of open water close by, possibly to the north.

As we travel side by side through life, Bill and I make a solid team.

Fog forms when frigid air temperatures meet warmer water. Because of the constant movement of the sea ice, wide cracks and sometimes persistent or permanent areas of open water exist in both summer and winter. Called "polynyas," and caused by currents, wind, and warm upwellings, these are treasure chests of wildlife, including seals. And of course, where there are seals, there are polar bears. Thus our surroundings provided plentiful clues about the conditions ahead.

As we fumbled our way along, Charlie suddenly stopped, his tail gently waving back and forth. He yipped twice and was answered by several wolf yips close by to our right. Then, with his head proudly erect, Charlie stepped in front to lead us, as if to display his alpha status. We suspected that these were wolves who already knew us.

Not being able to see them was spooky, but knowing they were close by provided a certain sense of companionship. We never felt threatened. They might have been following us out of natural curiosity, we speculated; the possibility that they were following a bear also occurred to us. As there was nothing we could do about the latter, we decided that our only option was to rely on Charlie's highly tuned senses to warn us if we came too close to a bear.

Many times during past expeditions, a problem had cropped up that we were powerless to solve. We soon learned that all we could do was keep going and work through it as we went, rather than stop and allow ourselves to become paralyzed with paranoia. Judging by Charlie's occasional glance to his right during the next hour and his tail fanning in acknowledgment of wolves unseen, we guessed that we were somehow paralleling their path across the ice. Considering what we had learned last summer about wolves' intense curiosity and Charlie's friendly, relaxed gestures, we were convinced that we were being accompanied by wolves and not bears.

Finally, a mile from the coast of Pullen Island, we again traveled over thick, solid ice. Our progress was still agonizingly slow as we groped our way along, frequently consulting our compass and GPS unit.

The ice showed frequent splits. Now and then the pack ice shuddered, toppling large chunks of ice. Gaps widened as we crossed, then dropped the ends of our sleds into the inky water as we hastily pulled them to safety. The ice taunted us with heart-stopping cracks, high-pitched whines, and *pings* that erupted from the depths.

We skied another half mile to where the surface appeared more stable, and camped there. Troubled by the unpredictable movement of the ice and the unrelenting fog, we ate a cold dinner without lighting the stove in case conditions worsened, forcing us to leave in a hurry.

Halfway through dinner, the distant rumble of breaking ice grew louder. We scrambled out of the tent. The sound seemed to come from the west, but the fog muffled everything, making it difficult to determine the exact direction. In case another major ice breakup was on its way, we loaded the sleds and set a course to the east, adrenaline speeding us away from the ominous sound.

Bill led, and as I skied practically on his heels with Charlie at my side, I suddenly paused to look behind me. I had heard a *swish, swish* and was sure that another skier would emerge from the gray gloom. But no one was there. Bill had also heard the sound and stopped.

Mystified, we concluded that the ice was playing one of its never-ending series of tricks on us. *Swish* was just another word in its vocabulary. All around us it quivered. A four-foot pinnacle fell over. We skied onward as the mysterious nonexistent skier kept pace. Frequently exchanging leads in the increasingly rough terrain, we took turns scouting for the best route.

Suddenly the ice split. Ice towers crashed around us. A pulsing vibration swept through the fog. We wanted to run but there was nowhere to go. We were in the midst of an ice eruption. Frightened, we ripped off our skis and lashed them to our sleds. I kept a firm, protective grip on Charlie's leash as he pressed hard against my leg, telling me he was afraid.

The distant rumbling, now much louder, closed in on us. I stared at sections of falling ice as though hypnotized. Time stood still as my heart tried to hammer its way out of my chest. A crack in the ice zigzagged past us, widening to three feet. Then a ghostly moan came from the direction of a pressure ridge we had just crossed. As we watched in disbelief, the entire thing collapsed on itself with a thunderous roar, sending blinding particles of snow dust into our faces. A hundred feet away, a flat area suddenly erupted upward under powerful pressure from the ocean depths. Plates of ice rose and slammed on top of each other. We hurdled a wide crack. In front of us a ridge jerked fifty feet apart.

Bill yelled, "Run!"

We haul our sled up and over the teetering blocks of ice.

The three of us raced for the opening with Charlie in the lead. We escaped across an ice bridge just before tons of ice slammed behind us. Dashing across a smooth spot, we leaped over a three-foot chasm, dunking the tails of our sleds into the dark water as we barely made it to solid ice.

Vibrations pulsed through our bodies. We were in the path of a freight train with no escape. To our left, ice spanned a twenty-foot-wide water lead. Bill went first, then Charlie, then me; but just as I lunged to safety the bridge fell, dragging the tail of my sled into the water. I had made it by a microsecond.

We searched for safety and escape, dodging violent eruptions and widening cracks. Charlie moved in unison with us.

After what seemed an eternity, the deafening noise slowly faded into the distance. We collapsed onto our sleds, emotionally and physically drained. Even a visiting polar bear would not have impressed us after our close call. We were thankful to be alive.

After we were sure the danger had passed, we looked for a suitable campsite as dusk settled around us. The fog had thinned, with visibility improving to five hundred feet.

The ice was still in such upheaval, though, that we could find no place to pitch our tent. There was nothing to do but press on, which meant attacking the pinnacles, the ice blocks and ridges carved into an endless array of abstract shapes that blocked our path in all directions. An hour later, nearing exhaustion, we were still struggling to heave our sleds up and over yet another ridge and through more teetering ice blocks. Even Charlie was tired. Darkness had descended, leaving only the reflection from the ice to give us a little gray light.

But now the stiff breeze became a strong wind that blasted our bodies with waves of spindrift. Snow forced its way down our collars and into the smallest openings in our clothing. Our jackets, masks, and parka hoods caked up and turned rock hard. A layer of ice covered Charlie's thick coat, and his face was a white mask.

The fog disappeared in the gale, but in our new misery we hardly noticed. Cresting another pressure ridge, we saw a level place ahead. We aimed for it, and although it turned out to be a sloping ice pan, it was the best we had seen in a long time.

The strong gusts tore at the tent. Bill threw himself across the flapping fabric while I grabbed the ice screws and fixed them into the cement-hard ice. The wind howled at us in the darkness. Just as my fingers turned numb, the screws went in and we shoved the tent poles through their sleeves. After we anchored the sleds close to the door, all three of us fell inside to begin the warming process.

After much windmilling of my arms, my fingers throbbed with the excruciating pain of returning circulation. Bill's hands had not fared much better, but as he gritted his teeth through the agony of warming, he knew his fingers were safe from severe frostbite. Charlie shook himself free of snow and ice, but at least he showered it near the door.

After I swept the snow into the vestibule, we unloaded our sleeping gear and food from the sleds. Finally everything we needed was inside. We lit the stove, cooked rice and instant potatoes, and ate dinner. Now warmer, reasonably well fed, and in our sleeping bags, we looked at our watches. It was 2 A.M.

"What a day," I mused. "Sometimes I wonder why in the world anyone would ever want to live like this."

"Makes the red blood cells wake up," was Bill's understated reply.

As we finished the last crumbs of our day's ration of food bars, we talked about how scared we had been. The adrenaline rush caused by the terrifying events had pushed us to react instantly, but it had also pushed us to an emotional edge, where only the instinct to survive had forced us to keep going rather than shut down in panic.

Later I wrote in my journal: "Today I have been scared to death. My heart beat so strongly it's a wonder it's in a fit condition to continue. Dodging for our lives does not impress me as a relaxing pastime. My prayers are for smooth skiing and unlimited visibility in bright sunshine. And no polar bears."

After further reflection on our day, I added: "Fear is a strange thing. I'm more convinced than ever that conquering fear isn't about bravery, but rather about how we handle it. If we had panicked we might have been killed, but the extreme adrenaline rush gave us the advantage to think at top speed and react as never before. Fear is like a wall. To survive, we forced our way through the wall that engulfed us and reached down into our innermost souls. We emerged with the ability to react in a way we had not known was possible."

As I set about the task of moving Charlie off my sleeping bag, I said to Bill, "I hope we're never tested like that again."

I thought of home and all our animals—goats, sheep, alpacas, donkeys, cats, and dogs. They seemed so far away. I missed them. But this train of thought would only get me into trouble, I knew. I switched my thoughts to memories of the wolves we had come to see and concentrated on the many tender sights we had witnessed, such as the limping female's companion taking care of her. My sadness evaporated. I thought of dear old Beta and all the summer wolves we had come to know so well. In my mind's eye I could see Alpha and Denali roving over the snowy tundra. The pups would be following, no doubt with Beta and Mother keeping an eye on them. I took the small brown rock from my pocket and again pressed it to my lips in silent prayer. My optimism was back.

My attempt to shove Charlie over and claim my full share of our bed was a complete failure. He merely spread out, lay his head on me, and went to sleep. I gave up and slid into the narrow sliver he had left for me.

We fell asleep to the sound of a wild storm, which now that we were safely in our tent was music to our ears because we knew the wind would push the fog away. At 5 A.M. we both awoke to silence. Unzipping the door, we looked out—only to be greeted by the same old fog. I prayed that by daylight it would be gone. And indeed, at 8 A.M. a gentle breeze tugged at the tent walls. The fog had thinned rapidly. We ate breakfast and packed, delighted.

Our late start rewarded us with an expanded world of blue skies and visibility that stretched to the horizon. But as we took in the view, our suspicions were confirmed. Ahead along our route, only a half mile away, was a vast area of open water.

A shadow spreading across the pale sky signaled the reflection of the dark open sea. As we closed in on the chasm, it showed itself to be more than a mile long and at least half a mile wide, displaying the typical green-black color of frigid Arctic water. Six polar bears paced along the its edges, hunting seals as arctic foxes and two wolves we recognized as Smudge and Crab kept close watch, hoping to share in the bounty. One bear saw us and approached, but after he satisfied his curiosity he returned to the water. Another two wolves who resembled the immature members of the sea ice pack watched us suspiciously, then turned back to keep an eye on the bears, who might provide a meal at any moment.

Twelve foxes scurried around, some with noses close to the ice, picking up what seemed to be tantalizing scents. Normally curious, they paid no attention to us. Charlie stopped to look the scene over, then raised his muzzle to catch the scents too. After sending a few yips of greeting to the wolves, he walked on without so much as another glance in their direction. He had apparently concluded that the bears were busy and had no interest in us. We could not bring ourselves to be quite so casual, though, and kept a wary eye on them just in case.

Taking a more southerly route to avoid the water, we found ourselves skiing over ice that, although jumbled in places, was the best skiing we had so far encountered. In another mile we noticed a bear three hundred feet ahead, feeding on a seal. Patch stood close by, as if waiting for his chance to share the meal. But the bear replied with a loud growl whenever the wolf took a step forward. At two hundred feet away, we stopped. Charlie, although interested, showed no alarm. The bear concentrated on his meal and the wolf who might steal it.

Soon Patch lay down and seemed content to wait. After consuming more than half the carcass, the bear withdrew a few feet and sat to lick his paws. Patch dashed forward to rip chunks of meat from the seal and gobble them down, as if worried that the bear might change his mind. Indeed, in several minutes the bear rose and, after a short growl, resumed his meal while Patch again retreated and watched. This time the bear finished off the seal except for a few small pieces. Apparently satisfied, he walked toward the open water and allowed Patch to eat the last bits.

On this journey we had encountered several members of the sea ice pack spread several miles apart. By instinctive reasoning they had apparently established that it was wise to spread out and follow different bears to share food. The earlier episode in which we met all eleven wolves in one place indicated that the family met occasionally in sheltered areas, perhaps to escape the full brunt of storms when hunting was impossible. After observing the playful intelligence of the summer pack, we wouldn't have been surprised if the sea ice group also gathered to exchange news and catch up on games.

We had detected the interaction of two major Arctic predator species, both intelligent hunters with a need to find prey wherever they could in the harsh conditions of the ice pack. That the polar bears shared their seal kills demonstrated the ability of both species to understand the needs of the other. Now we had observed winter and summer wolves as both groups shared food and established at least a primitive interspecies emotional bond and communication.

Our next task was to travel to the delta and the place John had marked on our map, where he had often watched a family of wolves gather at a winter meeting place. Our hope was that they would add to our knowledge of the ways wolves live in both summer and winter in the wild.

Camp

To avoid the water and reach smoother ice, we skied in a southeasterly direction toward the Canadian coast. Charlie caught the scent of another seal lair hidden beneath the ice surface and dug down, but its owner had left, probably at the first sound of the intruder.

Dangerous ice conditions had tested us almost to our limit, leaving our nerves taut. After two weeks on the sea ice, I craved the feel of solid land beneath my skis. We skirted east to find a dry route around more open water. The violent breakup had completely changed the surface of the ice since we had traveled across it on our way north. Newly formed ridges and recently opened areas of water blocked our path. We swung southwest to follow the Canadian coastline all the way back to Tuk.

After a day of uneventful hard skiing, we reached the coast not far from Tuk and stepped onto land, relieved to leave the sea ice behind. No more ice breakups, open water, polar bears, or long detours. We were eager to locate the wolves' gathering place on the delta that John had so enthusiastically described.

After setting up camp three miles outside Tuk, we took inventory of our supplies. In spite of the frustrating delays over the last twenty-seven days, we had more than enough provisions and stove fuel left to complete our trip even if our planned thirty-day expedition extended to sixty days. Charlie's dry dog food supply was ample at two pounds per day. Our equipment, which had taken a savage beating on the sea ice, had survived in reasonable condition.

The noisy arrival of two snowmobiles from Tuk put an abrupt end to the silence. Sitting astride their idling yellow and black Polaris machines, the young Inuit men introduced themselves as Mark and Tommy. Mark, probably in his twenties, with broad shoulders and powerful arms, lisped slightly through the gap where his two front teeth should have been. Tommy, of similar age, tall and slender, wore a perpetual smile on his ruddy-cheeked face. Arched eyebrows accentuated his conversation. After they scrutinized our gear and the supplies we had already laid out, Tommy emphatically proclaimed that he could see a serious need for more cookies, bread, and breakfast cereal.

"Give us fifty dollars and we'll bring back good food," Tommy said.

Bill handed over the money. With a roar, they throttled their machines across the snow toward Tuk.

"What the heck," Bill said as we watched them disappear. "Even if we don't see our money or the food, they were a cheery pair."

Two hours later we were pleasantly surprised to hear the two men racing back across the snow toward our camp. Mark towed a six-foot long wooden sled called a *komatik*. Tommy proudly pulled back the tarpaulin to display an array of food topped by twelve large chocolate bars. Then he unwrapped a newspaper parcel of muktuk, the blubber of beluga whales. We had tasted muktuk, a standard Inuit food, on a previous northern journey. Now just the oily smell of it made our stomachs turn. It was too much for our *kabloona* stomachs, even though it contains the health-giving omega-3 fatty acids so important in the fight against heart disease.

Previous generations of Inuit were far healthier than today's people. True hunter-gatherers, the traditional Inuit ate large quantities of seal and beluga meat and blubber in addition to other foods taken from the sea and land. The introduction of white people's foods such as sugar, margarine, dairy products, and candy, in addition to abundant supplies of alcohol and tobacco, have caused a steady decline in Inuit health. Tooth decay, obesity, heart disease, emphysema, and diabetes are common.

"We thought you'd like these after your dinner," Tommy said, pointing to the chocolate bars with his sparkling smile.

"Here's your change." Mark handed Bill twenty-one dollars. After Bill refused to take it, Mark turned to me. "Missus, you take it."

"No, it's yours," I said.

Mark waved his hand toward both purring machines and replied with a grin, "They do get hungry. Thanks."

After we unloaded the supplies, both men gunned their engines to circle our tent and, with a final dramatic salute, roared away to Tuk.

We packed the six loaves of bread, fifteen boxes of some type of nondescript crunchy cereal, and four large sacks of frosting-covered vanilla cookies into stuff sacks to load onto our sleds. The bread would automatically freeze, preserving it. Broken into pieces, it would make a fine addition to our dinner soup.

Bill chewed a slice of fresh bread and nodded his approval. "It's good."

Knowing we could never eat the muktuk, I gave some to Charlie, who gobbled it in seconds and looked for more. Clearly the smelly blubber wouldn't go to waste. I wondered if it reminded Charlie of his life in the North, before I met him, when all he ate was seal and whale. I put the rest in a safe place on my sled to ration it to him over the next several days.

Under more blue skies and a light wind, the temperature at -21 degrees, we set out to find the delta wolf pack. Four willow ptarmigan leaped into the air. The sudden throb of their wings startled us, while Charlie boisterously charged to the end of his leash. But the wily birds landed safely in another thicket, chattering in high-pitched, indignant voices. Although brown in summer, their plumage turned white in winter, making it the

In the delta camp, Mackenzie approaches and turns toward me,
suspicious. This animal is clearly the Alpha.

perfect camouflage against foxes and snowy owls. These tough
birds don't migrate for the winter; instead they burrow into the
snow, where the temperature is several degrees warmer than
outside.

The next night, as we wrote in our journals in the dim light
of a tiny candle that threatened to go out at any moment, we
noticed a laserlike beam of light penetrating the tent walls. In a
minute we were outside, gasping at the sight above us.

The northern lights, or aurora borealis, sent an immense curtain of soft green light pulsating across the sky, wavering in deli-
cate curves as if it were a bridal train filling the heavens, swirling
and moving to a silent script. A soft rose color gradually washed
across the green, only to retreat slightly, as if to share the uni-
verse with the green that now pulsated in unison with the rose.
Although the lower edge of these auroral displays usually does
not reach closer than a hundred miles above the surface of the

earth, the bottom of this one seemed to brush the horizon; at the top, the lights curved out to the infinity of space.

The northern lights are caused by charged particles that penetrate the atmosphere along the magnetic fields of the polar regions, creating a solar wind circling the earth at high latitudes. The enormous wall of light, sometimes several hundred miles long and at times more than 150 miles high, moves in waves across the heavens.

Mesmerized, we ignored the chill of the night air. The pulsating curtain drifted away as if to leave us, only to return, all the while moving back and forth in great folds and curves. Eventually, as the light faded to a dark sky full of stars, we returned to our sleeping bags, cold but in awe. Of all the auroras we had seen, this was probably the most spectacular.

Although short on sleep, we rose at dawn. In a biting twenty-mile-per-hour wind, we skied across the willow-covered coastal areas to reach the delta's interior in four days. The wilderness here remained in deep winter's brittle grip. Still at least five days from Inuvik at the end of February, we arrived at the place John had marked with a large black X on our map.

We saw a lone wolf track, but no wolves. Charlie zealously pressed his black nose into the hand-size paw prints, then aimed his head at the sky and howled with delight. He waited, as if expecting an answer, but there was only silence.

We skied toward a few wind-tormented trees, crossing more wolf tracks. Most looked old, but a few still retained the sharp edges of new prints. Charlie stopped twice, head tilted to one side, listening. Later, closer to the trees, he howled again. A short cry came from our left but stopped midnote, to be taken up moments later by several blended voices from deep within the shadows of the trees.

We reached a meager forest on higher ground. Close by, we pitched our tent on a patch of flat tundra with a view of the open delta, its immensity surrounding us on three sides, enfolding us in the serenity of isolation. Behind us in the fading light, the ghostly shapes of the forest were reflected in the snow. The ice road lay several miles away. We had seen no sign of snowmobiles or their tracks for days.

While we erected the tent, Charlie scent-marked several wolf tracks that crisscrossed the snow. So far we hadn't sighted a wolf, but the air was thick with their presence. As soon as the tent was up I stood aside, expecting Charlie's customary beeline inside for my sleeping bag, but he was preoccupied with carefully marking a roughly circular perimeter about fifty feet away.

He inspected the entire site, then scent-marked the tent on three sides. "Oh boy, here we go again," Bill said.

With his territory adequately claimed, Charlie sat expectantly outside the tent door, waiting for the visitors he seemed certain were close. After an hour we glimpsed a lone wolf gliding through the deep shadows of the forest.

At midnight, under another tapestry of northern lights that lit up the sky, Charlie stepped outside and aimed an intense stare at the area to the right of our tent. As we followed his gaze, we detected a slight movement. Charlie howled. Minutes later came a single call, then quiet yips, from a second wolf. They seemed so close that I looked around, half-expecting to see one at my side.

After a few minutes of quiet, Charlie returned inside, and we followed. But sleep didn't come easily when we knew that wolves were watching us from trees only two hundred feet away.

Next morning in the early light, a sudden chorus erupted. Six wolves stood at the edge of the forest, howling. The moment we stepped out of the tent, they stopped abruptly and then silently exchanged stares with Charlie. Within seconds Charlie sat down with his head turned to the side to avoid direct eye contact. We settled on our sleds and looked away submissively as well. First one wolf moved a foot closer; then another stepped forward. They froze in place when we looked directly at them, then relaxed as we feigned indifference.

The six quietly spread out, but remained close to the security of the woods. They moved without aggression, only with the curiosity we had also observed in the summer wolves. But their curiosity was tempered by nervousness as they eyed Bill and me sitting motionless on our sleds.

After a few minutes Charlie rose, tail curled high above his back to signal his alpha status over his human pack, just as he had with the summer wolves. He immediately became the sole focus of attention. A male, mostly blond with gray markings, approached alone, stiff-legged and cautious, to sniff and then resniff Charlie's painstakingly laid-out scent marks. After marking some with his own scent, as an added gesture of dominance the wolf defecated on a scent mark, then returned to his family, who had watched from the trees. This animal was clearly their alpha.

After an hour of strutting, renewing scent marks (including those on our tent), and yipping occasionally, Charlie, with a hint of arrogance, turned his back and strolled into the tent. He reappeared a few minutes later, still under the intense scrutiny of the wolves, none of whom ever took their eyes off the tent when Charlie disappeared. The dominant male again faced Charlie, but now slowly waved his tail. Charlie replied with a gentle fanning of his own tail. The two appeared to have agreed to be friends. We were ecstatic: This was the pack John had described and their acceptance of Charlie would allow us to remain in the area to observe them. To signify the end of the visit, Charlie re-entered the tent and lay down in his customary place across my sleeping bag, while the alpha, finding himself ignored, led his pack into the woods.

Now that we had established contact with the pack, we reread the notes John had written about his experiences and what we might expect from these delta wolves. His sudden switch from hunting wolves for their pelts to looking for wolves, as he told us, "just to be around them," had caused him to travel widely over the boundless delta.

A dedicated loner from Cambridge Bay farther east on the northern coast, John had no family ties in Inuvik. He had traveled north after leaving his job in Whitehorse and fell in love with the wide-open space of the delta. He passionately traversed the frozen waterways, forests, and willow thickets on his snowmobile looking for wolves, and in the process developed an intricate knowledge of the territory.

Four years ago he had camped close to our present tent site to wait out a brief snowstorm and discovered wolves living in the shelter of the nearby trees. They stayed for several days before heading across the delta to hunt. He followed at a discreet distance to avoid spooking them. After losing sight of them several times over hills and in trees, he caught up just as they chased down an aging caribou. They gorged themselves, then slept curled up in the snow. After another three days of hunting, much to John's surprise, they returned to where he had first seen them and stayed for three days. He camped a half mile away and kept watch with binoculars from a rise in the tundra.

Led by an alpha male and female, the family repeated the cycle throughout the winter. With spring's first signs of thaw, they disappeared into the hills south of Inuvik, where John suspected they denned, ready for the new season's pups. Although he searched, he never found their den. They repeated the same hunting and resting cycle each winter. Their numbers remained between six and ten, with some young adults dispersing.

Once John watched a fight between a midpack wolf and a stranger, a large dark gray animal. The fight to the death was won by the strange wolf, who continued to live on the fringes of the pack for several weeks. Eventually he challenged the leader. After a brief fight the leader ran for his life. That night, mournful howling filled the air from a distance. The alpha female left immediately, presumably to join her mate. Then the howling stopped, and John never saw either wolf again.

The stranger took over the position of alpha and bonded with a midpack female, who became the alpha female. John described him as dark, young, powerful, and extremely dominant. He was still the alpha in late January, when John had last visited the area.

One thing in John's notes puzzled us: The alpha leader he described was nowhere in sight. Leadership had changed. The alpha we now faced was lighter colored, looked laid-back, and appeared to rule with serene control. Rather than having lost a leadership fight, we speculated, the alpha John had seen had probably died from injury or disease. Perhaps this new alpha had been the family's beta wolf and had automatically stepped up in rank when his leader died. The present alpha—Mackenzie, as we chose to call him—was far less assertive than Alpha of the summer pack. He reminded us of lovable, calm Beta, who taught

A yearling bear enjoys a back scratch on the ice while his mother hunts at the water's edge.

the pups and disciplined the teenagers with the same gentleness we saw in Mackenzie.

We were sure that Charlie had confirmed his dominance over Mackenzie when we saw him turn his back on his visitor and enter the tent to abruptly conclude the visit. His actions demonstrated that he had a stronger personality than Mackenzie, whose manner was reflected in the behavior of his family. In our first encounter with the summer pack the entire group had stepped boldly forward, their posturing demanding a reason for our presence. But the delta group had stayed back, allowing Mackenzie to do all the investigating. When we first met the delta family, Charlie had no need for lengthy bouts of posturing and submission, a striking contrast to our initial rendezvous with the summer wolves.

Now that a positive relationship had been established, the wolves occasionally appeared at the edge of the trees and watched us. Haughty Charlie occasionally afforded them an indifferent glance; he seemed to make a point of showing them that he would communicate only on his terms.

At the end of the first day's contact, as darkness fell and a chill wind sent icy fingers down our parkas, we ate dinner and retreated to the warmth of our sleeping bags. We were thrilled about the day's events. A successful connection with a third wild wolf pack, in addition to the summer family and the sea ice pack, was beyond anything we could have wished for. We owed a great debt to John, who, once he understood that we would never harm the wolves, unselfishly shared the vital information that helped us find this delta pack. We eagerly looked forward to when he would visit us on the delta, as he had promised.

That night Charlie awakened us around midnight. We strained to hear what had roused him. Soft, careful footsteps crunched in the snow outside, accompanied by loud, inquisitive sniffs at the base of the tent walls. The wolves were inspecting our shelter.

Charlie sent a low *woof* into the night. In response came a barely audible whine, followed by more sniffing, louder whines, and several whimpers. Charlie continued with gentle *woofs*. The sounds were not those of begging or injured animals, but the language of communication at close quarters in the wild—perhaps even of submission. Could Charlie's dominance have won him such respect from these wolves so soon, even as their curiosity drove them to inspect the tent? We sat tense, still as stone, our ears tuned to the slightest sound, not sure what to expect.

Charlie made no attempt to go outside and, as usual, appeared in complete command of the situation. The wolves had crossed Charlie's well-marked perimeter, but he didn't behave defensively. He appeared to feel no need to prove his position of dominance with this family. In contrast, when the summer wolves had trespassed, he had angrily sent them packing to reinforce his reign over his own territory. Anything less would have shown weakness and decreased his neighbors' respect for him.

Mackenzie and his family eventually departed—satisfied with their findings, we hoped. It was early morning before we finally stopped talking about the delta wolves. Encouraged by Charlie's positive relationship with the delta wolves, we decided to establish Wolf Camp Two here and stay for about one month, until early spring. The pack's apparent calm gave us hope that the family would keep to the cycle John had described. If they showed signs of spooking, we would move our campsite farther away.

When we awoke, the only signs of the wolves were their enormous prints in the soft snow surrounding our tent. Late on the fourth day after their disappearance, we heard a distant howl from across the forest. Charlie, clipped to his leash to prevent him from dashing off to join the wolves, immediately replied. Fifteen minutes later another howl, much closer to our camp, elicited a second reply from Charlie. Soon the same six wolves stood at the edge of the forest, staring at us.

This pack of six was the smallest of the three families we had encountered. The summer pack had had eight members and the sea ice family, eleven. As we had done in the summer, to aid identification we chose names for the six. Mackenzie was named after the river that flowed through the delta.

A medium-size blond female and close companion of Mackenzie was intensely jealous of any female who dared approach her "man." She snarled and snapped a warning and drew blood one day when she chased another female and nipped her rump. The younger wolf immediately flipped onto her back in a submissive apology. The aggressor was the alpha female. We named her Willow.

Wolves become sexually mature at two years of age and breed from late January to mid-March. The more northerly wolves in colder climates mate later than their southern relatives, so that pups are born in warmer weather. As we approached the end of February in the breeding season, Willow protected her breeding rights with the alpha male by preventing any other female from having close contact with him. Mackenzie, in turn, discouraged the other males from any close association with his breeding partner.

Although the protective behavior produced more conflict than we had observed during our time with the summer pack, we never saw any fights or seriously aggressive acts. A simple rebuff appeared all that was necessary to maintain breeding rights and family harmony.

There were two other adults, both midpack animals. The female, who was almost white, we named Spruce. Her coat had an ungroomed appearance, mostly because its white color showed every bit of dirt. Her ruff was shaggy. She was a playful wolf who often cavorted through the trees carrying a stick and teasing another into trying to take it away. If successful in finding a playmate she would race away, weaving through the trees, kicking up snow at her heels, daring her pursuer to catch up.

We named the male Birch. He was gray with black streaks and a crooked tail, which we guessed had been injured in a hunting accident. He was a serious fellow, but often played with Spruce. Although not as quick at turning, he made up for his slower speed by intelligently cutting corners and ambushing Spruce from behind a tree. When the group set out on a hunt, Birch usually followed immediately behind Mackenzie, as if he were the second in command on hunts.

The two other wolves were younger. They were probably that year's pups, now almost grown but lacking the mature, well-rounded appearance of an adult. Richard, a male we named after Richards Island on the coast, was a well-proportioned animal with a gray coat and an unusual blond ruff. His stare, although not threatening, was intense. One day he would become an alpha.

His sister, Kendall—whom we named for the Kendall Island Bird Sanctuary, north of our position—was less intense than her brother. She seemed almost scattered when she played tag among the trees. Sometimes she stopped to peer around with a "Where did they go?" look. Then, seeing her quarry, she would race toward it full speed with long, bounding strides. Her lithe body destined her to become a speedy hunter.

After three days of resting and playing, the family disappeared during the night after hearing a bull moose trumpet in the distance. The only other sounds were the quiet whispers of a light breeze in the soft moonlight. Two days later the pack returned during a snowstorm, all with full bellies from successful hunts. They dug down into the snow and each curled up in a hollow, allowing the new snow to cover them for warmth.

Beneath their snowy mounds the wolves slept. Hours later, the snow stopped and the sun struggled through gray clouds. Mackenzie rose and stretched, shrugging the snow from his body, then sat on his haunches and yipped his family awake. They uncurled, breaking the layer of caked snow that covered them. One by one they rose to shake themselves free. Cavernous mouths agape, they yawned sleep away. Mackenzie and Willow greeted each other with soft muzzle caresses; then, together, they strolled closer to Charlie's boundary to peer at him sitting outside the tent, watching them. Spruce tried to initiate a game of chase, but the others were too lazy to respond, instead wandering into the trees to continue an idle day.

Mackenzie was the only one to approach our tent during the next several days. He gave Bill and me sporadic glances of appraisal, but it was clearly Charlie who fascinated him.

A steady cycle of hunting for a few days and returning to rest for one to three days continued. There must have been an abundant supply of large prey in the region to allow such a timetable, we reasoned. We had seen numerous groups of caribou and several moose on the delta.

Alone in camp one day, we heard the faint sound of a snowmobile. We hoped it was John, whom we had been expecting, and not hunters. Just in case, we implemented a plan we had discussed with him before we left Inuvik. As soon as the sound reached us, we clipped on skis and headed away from camp to intersect the snowmobile. If the visitors were hunters, we would tell them a story about "the wolves we saw yesterday going that way." Of course, "that way" would be in the opposite direction from where the delta wolf family rendezvoused.

Through binoculars we watched a black snowmobile disappear into a stand of spruce and a single figure begin walking toward us on snowshoes. It was John. We met up a quarter mile away. A man of few words, his greeting was short and to the point: "Hello, are the wolves there?"

After hearing a brief account of our adventures and of Charlie's success with the family, his eyes crinkled into slits as a wide smile spread across his weathered face. "Good news."

We continued on to our camp where John, who agreed to stay a few days, pitched his tiny green one-person tent beside ours. From his large, worn pack he took a sleeping bag with two rolled-up caribou skins lashed to the outside, and arranged them in the tent: one skin went under his sleeping bag, and the other was spread on top. John wasn't at all impressed with our foam sleeping pads. "*Kabloona* stuff is okay, but caribou skins are warmer." We made another trip back to his hidden snowmobile to carry his food to camp.

The next day the wolves returned. John, who had spent most of the morning sitting on a sled patiently waiting, didn't move. His body was relaxed, but his eyes sparkled as the wolves appeared at the edge of the trees. They immediately noticed him. Their heads went up; their ears pointed forward. In minutes they relaxed. He remained sitting perfectly still for another hour. Then, quite casually, he rose and said, "They know me."

Together we ate lunch and talked about the only subject John cared about: wolves. He was amused at the names we had given the family. It had never occurred to him to name them.

He was excited to hear of our contact with the family on the sea ice. In his travels to hunt seals, he had seen an unusual number of wolves on the ice for the past three years and had wondered if they stayed out there all winter. Now he had an answer.

As soon as John had arrived in camp, he noticed a change in Charlie, whom he had first met in Inuvik: "There he was a dog, now he's a wolf!" With his intimate knowledge of wild creatures, John instantly understood why we had been so successful in contacting wolves. He could see that Charlie was acting like a dominant wolf in the wild. After watching Mackenzie gazing at Charlie from his usual vantage point at the tree line, John chuckled and told us that Mackenzie was trying to imitate Charlie's sitting and standing posture.

John saw the wolves through the eyes of many generations of Inuit. He was able to look into their souls, to know them at a level we *kabloona* never could. He missed the dark alpha who had disappeared, and was visibly upset at the thought that a hunter might have killed him. It was more clear to us than ever that wolves were John's life.

Charlie's dominant, even pompous strutting captivated John. When Charlie looked at the wolves, John claimed that he could "see him talking to them with his eyes and body." Each day and late into the night, John sat silently watching Charlie and the wolves. Finally he asked us if we would consider leaving Charlie to live with him, so he and Charlie could travel together looking for wolves. John recognized that Charlie would be a bridge to the wolves for him, just as he had been for Bill and me. Charlie could pave the way for John to live closer to the animals he loved.

But John soon agreed that it wouldn't be possible. He sensed our unbreakable bond with Charlie, and knew he could never replace us. He knew Charlie's place was with Bill and me.

The delta wolves usually hunted at night, but early one morning, after a frenzy of howling, they left to hunt under a sky marked by threatening storm clouds. With John, we followed a narrow trail in the snow that led away from the forest, across the flat tundra, and over a low willow-covered rise. The wolves had traveled single file, stepping in the same tracks to save energy. Only the front wolf would break trail, and when he tired, another would take the lead. Their snowshoelike paws kept them on the snow's surface.

We cut across a frozen lake to a low hill as the wolves outdistanced us. From there we watched through binoculars as they chased a moose. They gave up after a short distance when the moose sped away on a frozen side channel of the river. The thin covering of snow over ice provided a firm footing for the speedy animal.

Undaunted, the hunters veered to the west and chased a caribou who made the mistake of breaking away from its main group. Caught in soft snow, the caribou floundered and soon went down under the mass of six wolves as its panicked companions dashed to safety. The wolves tore and slashed at the body, bolting down huge chunks of steaming meat with ravenous abandon. We were impressed by the wolves' efficient movement, even in snow— and especially compared to our more clumsy efforts. A cold seventeen-mile-per-hour wind picked up as we turned back to camp, leaving the wolves to eat and hunt.

We reached camp in time to escape the full strength of the storm, which built to a shrieking crescendo and kept us tent-bound for three days. Charlie, who clearly missed his new neighbors, stepped outside now and then, in spite of the tent-shaking winds, to see whether Mackenzie and his family had returned. But this time six days would elapse before they returned. We guessed that they had hunkered down in the storm and continued hunting after the weather cleared.

After spending ten days with us, John left to travel to the other side of the delta, where he thought he might see a few more of his wolf friends. He had been out on the delta for most of the winter, returning to town only to pick up his government check and buy supplies, and taking brief seal-hunting trips on the sea ice.

Even before John had agreed to tell us of the delta pack's location, we had promised to keep the rendezvous site's exact position a secret, just as for the summer pack. There was always the possibility that either pack, especially the delta one, might be found by hunters. Both families had given us so much. Anything that might lead hunters to them would be a betrayal to the wolves and to John.

We accompanied John to his snowmobile and agreed to meet him in Inuvik after we returned from the delta. As he drove westward in search of more wolves, we were sorry to see him go. His Inuit wisdom, quiet ways, and ability to understand Charlie's acceptance by wild wolves amazed us. His sense of "wolf language," as he called it, had given us greater insight into the wolves' thinking and Charlie's place in their lives.

Stranger

MARCH SLIPPED IN ON WARMER TEMPERATURES. As dawn made its appearance one morning, a solitary howl ending in a sorrowful wail carried across the tundra on the light breeze.

Six wolves were instantly at the edge of the trees, their triangular ears bolt upright, watching a single wolf approach slowly but steadily from a half mile away. The pack tensed as the stranger approached. He stopped now and then to howl tremulously, perhaps seeking permission to approach. Mackenzie stepped to the front of his family and howled briefly in response.

When the stranger, an immature male with a bloody shoulder, was three hundred feet from the pack, Mackenzie advanced, stiff-legged, his fur ruff raised. His lips drew back, exposing teeth set in powerful jaws, and a deep, angry rumble rose from his throat. The stranger's blood-covered shoulder was gashed, but his steady gait showed no limp. He stopped as Mackenzie drew close, then yelped and cowered in submission as the aggressive alpha steadily approached.

With a savage snarl, Mackenzie—his face contorted into a vicious mask, his ears pointing hornlike to the side—suddenly jumped to partially straddle the stranger, who immediately dropped to the snow and flipped onto his back, tail clamped tightly between his legs. Mackenzie stood over him, his fangs stabbing the stranger, snatching quick bites of fur. Then, after inspecting the stranger's genital and anal areas, he stepped back, still snarling. The stranger lay on his back, whining pitifully.

By now the entire family had approached and stood over the cringing wolf. Willow grabbed a mouthful of fur and yanked hard, pulling the prostrate wolf a few feet. The rest, snarling and biting, tormented the poor beast for several minutes, drawing blood from his rump and neck. Then, led by Mackenzie, the family withdrew to the tree line, leaving the young wolf groveling on his back.

Meanwhile, just as Mackenzie first advanced on the stranger, Charlie rushed to his scent marker closest to the scene to stand guard over his territory. He snarled a vicious warning to the stranger to stay back. Straining to the end of his leash, he breached his boundary to further emphasize his message. Even as Mackenzie led his family away, Charlie continued a rumbling growl. Bill and I, shotguns in hand, stood within a few feet of Charlie in case the stranger decided to fight the dog that confronted him.

The pack disappeared into the trees, but we suspected they still watched. It was an hour before the stranger slowly rose. Immediately all six wolves silently reappeared at the tree line. Charlie, who at our urging had retreated to the side of the tent, resumed his aggressive boundary stance: teeth bared, deep-throated snarls catching in his throat, facing down the bloodied wolf.

Slowly the wolf advanced, shying away from Charlie. Finally, only fifty feet away from Mackenzie, the wolf again cowered on the snow and whined. Mackenzie walked to him, this time without aggression, and sniffed his bloodied fur. He turned toward his family with the stranger walking behind: head down, back arched, and tail tightly tucked beneath his body. The family gathered about, sniffing and moving in short, sudden jumps: leaping sideways to the stranger, then jumping to the front to block him. Thirty minutes later they wandered away to resume family life, leaving him alone.

Stranger approaches.

Not so Charlie. Every time the stranger looked toward him, Charlie resumed an aggressive posture, snarling fiercely. The wolf seemed to have been somewhat accepted by the family, but not by Charlie.

The stranger lay a hundred feet away, cleaning his bloodied wounds. We were relieved that the possibility of a fight seemed to have evaporated. The stranger was gradually gaining acceptance, but we wondered whether the family would accept him as a pack member.

Night arrived with the stranger lying at the edge of the trees, still being ignored. Charlie had calmed and ceased to continually guard his territory. Concerned that the outsider might still be rejected by the pack, and troubled about the bites the family had inflicted on him, we looked out now and then. In the darkness all we could see was a form huddled in the snow, all alone. Charlie showed no interest.

At dawn the lonely animal was on his feet, but limping slightly. Mackenzie approached. The two gently touched muzzles and Mackenzie led the stranger into the trees—to where the family waited, we presumed.

Toward nightfall the family reappeared, with the newcomer following close behind. He appeared to have been accepted, although he carefully kept to the rear. We were thankful to see that he walked confidently and his limp had improved.

By now we had seen many instances in which wolves displayed intense emotions toward each other. Once the family accepted the newcomer, they demonstrated compassion toward him, as demonstrated by Mackenzie's soft muzzle touch, signaling acceptance. It was a glimpse of the gentler side of wolf family life.

Charlie's attitude was now one of complete indifference, as if his high status within the pack placed him above concern over a newcomer.

A day later all the wolves, including the outsider, left the area. Four days later they reappeared, the family's new addition bringing up the rear. His appearance had changed dramatically. His coat was clean, and he gave no sign of a limp. He held his head high and stepped along with a certain jauntiness. He had found a new family, and all was well in wolf town. Even Charlie allowed him a softer look as they passed by.

They all burrowed down in the snow to rest for the next several hours. After awakening with the usual long stretches and wide yawns, the stranger carefully approached Charlie's boundary, as if to make friends with the last holdout. Charlie at first simply watched him and then, just as with Mackenzie, he stepped inside the tent and ignored the stranger, who sniffed one or two markers and then discreetly retired to the forest.

It took me twelve journal pages to describe all that had transpired from the moment the newcomer had first appeared. Watching the acceptance of a stranger into the family circle was an unforgettable experience. "Just when we think we have seen everything in wolfdom," I wrote, "something happens to remind us that there will always be more to learn." In our notes we both referred to the new wolf as Stranger. We agreed that would be his name.

His immature body, exceptionally long-legged and large for his age, was covered in dense fur characteristic of that found on northern wolves, who must endure cold temperatures. His markings were typical of a gray wolf. Along his back and around his ruff, coarse, black-tipped guard hairs covered gray and white fur, giving his entire coat a gray cast.

As the days passed he played, but he always kept to the fringes. He didn't fit the role of omega, though. The family, which now numbered seven, accepted him as an equal and never picked on him, as they would have a true omega. Judging by his gashed shoulder, we guessed that Stranger had been driven forcefully from his pack and had traveled the delta alone, looking for a new family. Happily, he seemed to have found one.

Charlie leaps toward the stranger.

Affection

ONE EARLY EVENING IN MARCH, Birch, Spruce, and Stranger left to hunt in the south. An hour later Mackenzie and Willow and the two youngsters gathered for their ritual of excited muzzle licking and yipping. Soon they galloped away to the north. Two days later Spruce and Birch reappeared, each carrying a hare. Stranger followed, carrying part of a caribou hind leg.

Upon seeing that the rest of the wolves had left, they dropped their food and rushed back and forth through the trees, alternately voicing short alarm barks and yipping. The three distraught wolves appeared panicked that the rest of the family wasn't there to greet them. In unison they stood together at the forest edge and sent long howls into the dusk.

Minutes later a barely perceptible sound of howling reached our ears. The threesome howled again, their bodies quivering with tension. Another answer rode in on the wind from afar. Messages were sent back and forth for an hour, the distant howls coming closer with each chorus. Finally the four burst through the trees, to be greeted with happy bouncing, yips, and frantic muzzle licking.

Suddenly Spruce, Birch, and Stranger dashed to the food they had carried home and placed it at the feet of the returning foursome, who graciously accepted it, wolf style: by gulping it down. The four, although arriving without food in their jaws, had already eaten well, judging by their distended bellies. All seven then burrowed into insulated pockets of snow just inside the perimeter of the trees and slept away the next several hours. We never determined why the young threesome had panicked when they found wolf town empty.

Every time we saw wolves display their attachment to each other, we were reminded of the way that dogs bond to human masters. Dogs engage in the same body wriggling, licking, enthusiasm, and, most of all, boundless love. This is the core of pack bonding.

In fact, the more we learned about wolves, the more they reminded us of man's best friend. The domestic dog descends from the same genus (*Canis*) as the wolf. Both are meat eaters and highly social. Wolves and dogs breed together readily, even in the wild, with gestation time and litter size about the same. Both animals give birth to pups that are blind for the first days of their lives. A few differences are that wolves tend to have longer muzzles, thicker fur, and longer and far more powerful jaws than dogs, who lack the mile-upon-mile stamina of wolves.

Wolf-dog hybrids have become increasingly popular in recent years. (Since Charlie's wolf heritage stems from three generations back, he is mostly dog and could never be considered a true hybrid.) Because of the Inuit husky's distant link to the wolf, breeding the two creates a more compatible mix than the potentially unstable combination of a wolf and another breed of domestic dog.

Too often wolves are bred with domestic dogs selected for their aggression. Dogs exhibit far less control over their instincts than wolves, so such a union produces an animal that will fight to the death, whereas wolves will kill only what they can eat and will avoid danger if at all possible.

Lois Crisler raised wolves in Alaska in the 1950s and made significant contributions to wolf research. She bred wolves to dogs, hoping to produce animals more compatible to humans. The hybrids were more aggressive than wolves and seemed to suffer from an inbred schizophrenia resulting from the wildness

Charlie stares across the frozen delta hoping to sight caribou.

of wolves and tameness of dogs. She felt that the two opposite traits filled the animals with alternating rage and anxiety and could never be treated as dogs.

Some people try to raise wolf pups as pets, but as the adorable puppies grow they often become difficult to manage and end up in the backyard, permanently chained or caged. The highly sociable wolf part of the animal longs for the freedom to roam and hunt, to establish rank within a pack, and to enjoy the close-knit structure of a caring family. Instead, many captive wolves and hybrids turn into dull-eyed, pathetic creatures who know nothing but submission and torment as they are forced to obey human rules and accept confinement. If the animals become emotionally unmanageable, the owners surrender them to shelters, where they are often killed or turned loose into the wild without the skills to survive, causing them to attack dogs and domestic animals in their quest for food.

Over the weeks, when the pack wasn't hunting, Mackenzie spent an increasing amount of time watching Charlie. Sometimes he sat at the tree line and, although he never crossed Charlie's scent marks, he would wander along the boundary, sniffing here and there. There was a longing in Mackenzie's stare that we couldn't fathom, something far beyond the respect a subservient animal would have for a dominant alpha. We finally decided it was infatuation.

Charlie, for his part, grew less haughty and would sit alongside the tent, silently communicating with Mackenzie via an increasingly softer gaze. One of the many things we had learned during our year with wolves was that animals communicate with humans and each other on a level beyond words, and that human language is clumsy and limited compared to the emotional language of animals.

As mid-March approached, our rations were beginning to run low, even with the extra supplies Mark and Tommy had brought us from Tuk. We reluctantly acknowledged that we would soon need to leave the wolves, and began to prepare ourselves emotionally for another parting.

Perhaps the wolves caught wind of our thoughts. One day in the second week of March, Mackenzie stood in his usual spot a hundred feet away from us and howled, then whined softly, as he watched Charlie. He walked toward the trees, glancing back over his shoulder at Charlie, urging him to follow. Charlie, at the end of his seventy-five-foot leash, urinated on two of his scent marks, looked intently at Mackenzie, and then returned to the tent, giving him the same sort of looks. Each appeared to want the other to follow.

For some reason Mackenzie was attempting to entice Charlie to join him in the pack. But Charlie was steadfastly bonded to Bill and me. Instead, Charlie was trying to persuade Mackenzie to join *him*. After several minutes of unsuccessful efforts to persuade the other, they appeared to reach an agreement to enjoy each other's company from their own respective territory. Charlie possessively leaned on the tent, while Mackenzie calmly settled in the snow and cleaned his paws.

One moonlit 19-degree night in mid-March, the sound of thundering hooves awoke us. We leaped to the door as the tent was bumped by an unseen body. Grabbing the shotgun, Bill was first out the door, followed by Charlie and me.

Caribou swept past both sides of our tent, with seven wolves right on their heels. The frenzied caribou reached the forest at full speed and fled into the night. The hunters closed on a straggler. The sounds of leaping wolves and the desperate cries of an animal going down cleaved the still air. The wolves gorged themselves.

Charlie, caught up in the excitement, tugged hard at his leash. We pulled on our boots and allowed him to lead us closer to the feasting wolves, stopping a few yards away. Mackenzie looked up, saw that it was Charlie, and turned his attention back to gulping the meat.

Returning to the tent with a reluctant Charlie following, we discovered two bent pegs where the caribou had hit the tent. After Bill straightened them, we resumed our interrupted sleep. The next morning Charlie discovered a gift: A portion of the caribou's hind leg lay at his boundary. Mackenzie watched from the edge of the trees as Charlie picked it up, then lay alongside the tent to enjoy the fresh meat.

Three days later, an hour after the pack returned from a hunt, Birch left alone. He returned with a limp fox in his jaws and laid it on the snow. As he ate, he ignored the three youngsters, who groveled and pleaded for a share. After the entire carcass had disappeared, even the white furry feet, he walked away. The youngsters greedily licked blood from where the fox had lain. Perhaps it had been a deliberate lesson to the three young wolves to respect an older member. Soon Birch returned and initiated a game of chase. They all leaped and ran in wild circles with great grins on their faces, disappearing into the trees at top speed only to reappear in a burst of flying snow.

As the end of March approached, Mackenzie's apparent reluctance to dominate except when absolutely necessary, coupled with his desire to please Charlie, gave us more clues that eventually helped us solve the mystery of why Mackenzie would try to attract Charlie into the ranks of his family. The most obvious answer was that Mackenzie wanted Charlie, with his stronger personality and greater dominance, to take over as the family alpha, which would allow Mackenzie to return to the beta position.

Mackenzie's tranquil personality and intrigue with Charlie made it increasingly clear that he was not comfortable in the alpha position. We had earlier speculated that he would have functioned more happily in a beta midpack role, but had reluctantly stepped up the social scale to replace the family's lost leader.

The contrast between the personalities of Mackenzie and Alpha widened with the passing of winter. Alpha had been as strict as Charlie. With Mother, he had reigned supreme over the summer wolves. Although a beloved ruler, Alpha proudly relished the respect that his rank brought him. It was the only position he would tolerate. But Mackenzie, although the head male of his family, ruled in a less demanding way.

Stranger's integration into family activities appeared complete after three weeks. Once the ordeal of the initial submissive ritual was over, his life appeared more tranquil. He avoided Charlie's wrathful gaze for the first two weeks, but gradually plucked up enough courage to inspect his markers. Charlie watched, stiff-legged and challenging, unwilling to cut Stranger any slack. After the third week, though, Charlie relented. When Stranger approached the scent marks, Charlie treated him with the same haughty superiority he showed the other wolves.

Stranger was an intense animal, with a steady gaze that seemed to pierce our souls. He quickly assumed a dominant role with respect to the two other younger wolves, Richard and Kendall. His play was more gentle than theirs, but they and the rest of the pack developed a definite respect toward him, and over time his natural dignity and grace came to the fore.

One night the sounds of wolves again surrounded our tent. They sniffed and snuffled. One boldly scratched the wall close to where Charlie silently listened. He barked a single gruff challenge. The scratching immediately stopped. Soft crunching sounds faded away into the forest. The neighbors had obeyed Charlie's barked order to go home.

By the end of March the deep chill of midwinter had passed. Our rations were stretched to the limit. The wolves would continue their lives of hunting and returning to their resting area, but we could stay no longer.

We hated to leave, but knew we must. It seemed ages since we had set out last April, almost a year before, to travel to the summer den in the Yukon.

We waited until all the wolves had returned from a hunt before we took our tent down and loaded it onto a sled. As in the summer, we wanted the family to know where we had gone, especially because Charlie would have to abandon another group of companions.

While we packed our sleds, Charlie watched. Although subdued, he did not show the extreme sadness he had when we left Wolf Camp One.

Mackenzie and his family all watched from the trees. Charlie walked to his boundary and renewed a few scent marks, as if he didn't want his friends to forget him. He stood with his back to us and returned the family's stare. Mackenzie paced back and forth and quietly yipped. Charlie fanned his tail in conversation.

We finished securing our loads and clipped on our skis. As we had with the summer pack, we said good-bye to each individual and promised to return. Bill and I both cried as we skied away with Charlie's leash attached to my harness. He stopped to glance back at the wolves several times.

Willow stood at the edge of the clearing with the family, while Mackenzie followed a hundred feet behind our sleds. We climbed a low rise and descended the other side. Mackenzie stood tall and regal on the crest for several minutes, then slowly turned back to his family. It broke our hearts to watch him leave.

We skied single file, led by Bill. We were too choked up to talk. Charlie walked quietly at my side without looking back. I could feel his sadness, but he seemed to have accepted that we were going home.

An hour later, the wolves surprised us as they flitted through the trees to our left. Charlie stopped, sat on his haunches, and raised his muzzle in one last sorrowful howl to his friends, who answered with a long wailing chorus. Mackenzie had brought his entire family to say one last good-bye to Charlie.

With tears we bade our friends farewell again. Then Willow touched her shoulder gently to her mate's. Mackenzie, who had blossomed into a gentle if reluctant leader, turned and led his family away, with Willow close at his side. She seemed to know that Mackenzie longed for Charlie to stay, and comforted him with little brushes to his muzzle.

Our hearts heavy, we continued through the forest that now seemed terribly empty. But our hearts and minds were full of unforgettable memories and insights—many unexpected—that we had gained from our year with the wolves.

Epilogue

Passages

O UR YEAR WITH THE WOLVES immeasurably deepened our knowledge and appreciation of these much maligned animals. While wolves are often portrayed as villains—as in fairy tales such as *Little Red Riding Hood* and *The Three Little Pigs*—our experiences told a different story. We witnessed many acts of compassion and kindness in the three wolf families we observed. They had ample opportunity to attack us as we traveled among and lived close to them, had that been their true nature, but they did not.

Following our year of observation, we continued to visit the summer wolves every other year. To ensure that their familiarity with humans would not reach a level that might endanger them, we never again directly approached the den. Instead we observed them from a ridge downwind to ensure that we would remain undetected, the same ridge from which we had first surveyed them on our reconnaissance journey. The rocks easily concealed us, enabling us to camp with our sleeping bags on the ground for several days at a time.

We watched Beta, as gentle as ever with each set of new pups, for four years, after which we assumed he had passed on. The pack continued to be led by Alpha through the summer of 2001, but by 2003 a five-year-old gray-black wolf had adopted the alpha role. Meanwhile, the aging Alpha had taken over the beta role and appeared to be a respected elder just as Beta had been.

Mother remained the leading female for five years, after which her place was taken by a regal female who seemed to have joined the pack from another area. Mother seemed happy in her new role; we never observed any animosity as family social roles changed.

Yukon remained but Klondike disappeared, we assumed to find a mate and start her own family. Denali, although no longer the first to dash off to lead a hunt these days, is still hunting and spends long hours watching for prey from the ridge top. Omega now holds a midpack position and displays greater confidence. The two young, mischievous brothers grew into large and powerful, but still playful, adults.

Many pups have been born; some have stayed on and others have dispersed, bringing the total number of wolves in the family to sixteen. The wolves appear content to use the same den and surrounding rendezvous area year after year.

We also followed the delta wolves for the next three winters, traveling by snowmobile with John to visit them. We watched Stranger become the new alpha male, while Mackenzie seemed content in the role of beta; we believe he encouraged the change. Mackenzie's mate, Willow, appeared as devoted as ever, even though her position as alpha female was assumed by a new wolf. John surmised that the new alpha female had followed Stranger from his original pack to become his mate. Spruce, Birch, Richard, and Kendall remained with the pack and by 2002 the addition of new pups had raised the family's number to fifteen.

The delta wolves also faced a crisis that year. Oil and gas exploration on the delta had reached an intense level, bringing with it a dramatic increase in the number of heavy trucks that traveled the ice road. The invasion of the wolves' hunting range by humans caused the animals to become so distraught that John feared they would leave the area altogether.

All through January 2002, Stranger and Mackenzie rarely relaxed when the family returned to their winter rendezvous. John remained close by, camped in a spruce thicket all month without a break. His worst fears were realized in the first week of

February when, led by Stranger, the pack left for the rugged hills and valleys many miles southeast of Inuvik.

John followed on his snowmobile, sometimes keeping them in sight but mostly scouting their tracks in the snow. Throughout February, the wolves continually hunted and traveled throughout a wide range. By March, however, they seemed to have regained a sense of confidence and began hunting and returning at intervals to a sheltered valley, just as they had rendezvoused on the delta. That summer a delighted John discovered their den. He continues to observe the family from a distance, as he did on the delta.

Bill and I keep the exact location of the summer and delta wolves' den sites and rendezvous areas a well-guarded secret to avoid the possibility of leading hunters to the animals. All photographs in my public lectures and certain photographs in this book have been edited with security in mind.

🐾

Our time with the wolves also gave us a deeper appreciation of our beloved Charlie. We could never have successfully lived with the wolves without his unusual ability to gain their respect. His natural interaction with the inhabitants of the wild country was extraordinary.

Every time we visited the wolves to check up on them, Charlie accompanied us. As we observed from the ridge, he tugged at his leash, urging us to allow him to join the pack, and he was puzzled by our insistence that he remain hidden behind the rocks. By the second day, he seemed to accept that he had to observe from a distance, and set up a constant watch. Even though he could not join the family, he appeared happy to be near them once more.

Early on our first day of observation of the delta wolves Charlie gave a short howl when the family returned to their usual resting site. Mackenzie immediately stared across the void to where trees concealed our tents. He sent out a long howl in apparent recognition of Charlie and fanned his tail. Although we kept Charlie tethered at the side of the tent, out of sight of the wolves, he fanned his tail as Mackenzie voiced his recognition.

John, who was with us that day, observed the interaction and said quietly, "They'll be friends always."

🐾

In the years following the publication of *Polar Dream*, the story of my solo trek to the magnetic North Pole with Charlie, our gentle dog touched the hearts of thousands of people. He appeared at schools and events and on television shows such as *Good Morning America*. He visited nursing homes, children's hospitals, and camps for children with special needs. And he was the guest of honor at many fund-raisers for animal shelters.

Even today, fan mail from all over the world addressed to Charlie still arrives in a steady stream. His magnetism attracted people from all walks of life. Strangers would kneel to hug him. He imparted an angelic love that made people want to touch him.

Charlie celebrated his twenty-third birthday in 2003. His excellent health and long life were no doubt enhanced by strong genes, daily exercise, home-cooked food, and the monthly visits he enjoyed to his chiropractor and acupuncturist. But finally, his age caught up with him. Three weeks after we last visited the summer wolves, Charlie passed away peacefully in his sleep.

Although we miss him deeply, and will never really get over losing him, we cope by keeping him in our thoughts every day. We cherish every memory and everything he taught us. His soft gaze watches us from a life-size painting. We assume Charlie and Beta are howling happily together in heaven.

Charlie now lies at peace in a special place in a beautiful grove on our farm, overlooking the mountains he loved. He will always walk at our sides in spirit. His uncanny intelligence, along with his unfailing devotion to Bill and me, will continue to guide our path until we all meet again.

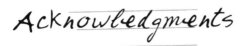

Acknowledgments

OUR MANY THANKS to our friend Marlin Greene of 3 Hats Design who has freely given of his advice and help. A thank you to John, our Inuit friend, who trusted us and allowed us into his world of wolves. Thank you, Margaret, for your unfailing support and encouragement.

Also thanks to my agent Anne Depue, and to Gary Luke and Heidi Schuessler of Sasquatch Books—and copyeditor Sherri Schultz—for your timely editing and suggestions.

And a special thanks to all those scientists who have provided information over the years concerning wolves and have created a solid base for my own wolf studies.

About the Author

HELEN THAYER was born and raised in New Zealand and graduated from Auckland University. She has been an international track and field athlete, and she won the U.S. women's national luge title in 1975 at age 36. When she was 50, she became the first woman to walk and ski to the magnetic North Pole; the account of that adventure became the book *Polar Dream*. She has received many awards and accolades for her adventures, including the Outstanding Achievement Award by the American Mountain Foundation (now the Rocky Mountain Field Institute). In 2002 Helen was named by the National Geographic Society/National Public Radio as one of the great explorers of the 20th century and was honored at a

BILL THAYER

White House reception by President Clinton for her expeditions and educational work. She is a regular speaker before organizations and corporate groups. She and her husband Bill live in the foothills of Washington's North Cascade Mountains.